HORNS UP, BOYS...

IT'S SHOWTIME!

JOHN HUGHES BENNETT

Horns Up, Boys… It's Showtime!
Published by Bennett Publishing
Fort Collins, Colorado

First Edition, September, 2020
ISBN: 978-0-578-74878-8
BIOGRAPHY & AUTOBIOGRAPHY / Music
MUSIC / Genres & Styles / Jazz

Cover and Interior Design by Victoria Wolf,
Wolf Design and Marketing

Author photo by Kathy Bennett

**BENNETT
PUBLISHING**

To Bill Hodges
(August 4, 1928–June 1, 2003)
An incredibly fine "first-call" lead trumpeter whose
impeccable playing helped define the top quality
performance synonymous with Las Vegas showbands.

This Book Is For
For my amazing wife Kathy, our terrific daughters
Kara, Lisa and Stacey, our wonderful grandchildren
Abigail, Emilie, Lucas, Dillon and Hali and super
energetic great-grandchildren Jayden and Mason and
another great-grandbaby soon to join our family.

CONTENTS

FOREWORD

THE HUMOR OF MUSICIANS has been a fun part of my 60-plus year career as a professional player. Oftentimes, many players, along with being creative musically, have equally creative minds when it came to comments and pranks. Hysterically funny, quirky, caustic, and "kidding on the square" are all words describing well a musician's offbeat slant on life.

Enormously talented jazz players such as violinist Joe Venuti, trombonist Bill Harris and trumpeter Jack Sheldon were world renowned for their hysterically funny onstage comments and pranks. Their antics and observations about fellow musicians offered much relief from tension and jangled nerves sometimes associated with live perfomance and recording.

With the gradual demise of big bands nation wide, and in particular in Las Vegas, many young musicians today may never have the opportunity to enjoy the wry sense of humor of some of these players. Before stories like these are lost forever, the goal is to preserve a few for future generations. In my being an active player for over thirty-three years playing over 20,000 shows in Vegas showrooms, there were many opportunities for me to witness firsthand events such as these.

With some stories being old, some new, some familiar, these then, with apologies to writer, Nathaniel Hawthorne, are my "twice told tales."

JHB
Fort Collins, Colorado 2020

CHAPTER ONE

LONG AGO AND FAR AWAY

"Jazz washes away the dust of everyday life."
—Art Blakey, drummer/leader,
"The Jazz Messengers"

CAN YOU IMAGINE IRONING your one clean gig shirt with a hot bulb from a hotel lamp? Or maybe pressing your black pants between the mattresses of a lumpy bed? At the same time, trying to scarf down a couple of dry bologna sandwiches and a cup of steaming hot coffee before hustling to a gig that paid only 50 cents a night plus a bowl of soup? Bandleaders were paid the princely sum of one dollar but they had to drive their own cars to the gig! Performing concerts at CCC Camps (Civilian Conservation Corps) around the country during the Great Depression helped many scuffling musicians put food on the table and hold it together.

If you can picture this scene, then you have recaptured the "glamorous" lifestyle of the road musician of the mid-1930s. "It's deja vu all over again," as Yankee catcher Yogi Berra once said.

*"I'm gonna put my shoes on backwards
and stride forward into the past."*
—Bill Harris, jazz trombonist

Despite, or because of, working conditions like these noted above, musicians have always been known for having a rather bizarre sense of humor. It seems to go well with the persona of a sideman. Many of these ex-road players who marched to their own rhythm eventually found their way to the bands and bright lights of Las Vegas.

One of the more famous, and certainly most

outrageous, of these was jazz violinist Joe Venuti, who appeared onstage in Vegas many times throughout his illustrious career. World renowned as a most creative jazz player and possessing a rare talent for practical jokes, Joe was featured during the late 1920s with Paul Whiteman's Symphonic Jazz Orchestra. This well-disciplined group featured, among others, such outstanding players, singers and future bandleaders as Bix Beiderbecke, Jack and Charlie Teagarden, Tommy and Jimmy Dorsey, Henry Busse, Bunny Berigan, George Gershwin, Bing Crosby, Johnny Mercer, Ferde Grofe' and of course, Joe Venuti. In bringing a sophisticated new kind of music to a wide range of audiences never before exposed to jazz, the Denver-born Whiteman enjoyed much fame being called "the King of Jazz."

For their many gigs, the orchestra was always attired quite properly in black ties and tails, with the rotund maestro dressed in a blazing all white tuxedo and white shoes. Wielding his two-foot long baton like a rapier, Whiteman ruled the orchestra with a strong hand and was well known for not having a keen sense of humor.

With a flair for the dramatic to prepare the audience for the entrance of the great Whiteman, the program, as usual, was begun each night with a loud timpani roll and a strong pedal note from the tuba, followed by the announcement. On one unforgettable night, Venuti could restrain the limits of his humor no longer. Furtively sneaking on stage a few minutes early, he emptied a 10 pound sack of flour down the bell of the old style upright tuba!

Needless to say, when the program began, the timpani roll sounded and the tuba loudly trilled its pedal note, the black suited orchestra was immediately showered with a blizzard of floating white flour!

Whiteman was flabbergasted, the orchestra stunned, and Venuti near hysterics with laughter.

"Never look at the trombones,
it only encourages them!"
—Richard Strauss, composer

As the announcer for "The Lone Ranger" radio show of the 1940s used to say: "Return with us now to those thrilling days of yesteryear," when air was clean and sex was dirty. Doing 1001 nighters on a band bus was certainly no picnic for the average young sideman back in "the good 'ol days" before the beginning of

World War Two. Hot bands of the day like Jean Gold-kette, Ben Bernie, The A&P Gypsies, Horace Heidt, The Clicquot Club Eskimos, and Lawrence Welk's Musical Syncopators traveled from coast to coast in bad buses on bad roads. No interstate highways available then. To escape the hazards of forever being a road rat, many players gravitated to the far west where work was more plentiful.

Las Vegas was on its way to becoming a mecca for musicians.

"Traveling with a big band is like being an inmate in a traveling zoo!"
—Hoagy Carmichael, "Stardust" composer

The Tommy Dorsey band, conducted after Tommy's death by durable tenor saxophonist Sam Donahue, was traveling through West Virginia on one of its many road tours, and had stopped at the single traffic light in a small town.

A little old lady approached the bus and started banging on the door saying, "I want to see Tommy. I want to see Tommy!"

Bandleader Sam opened the door and gently said, "I'm sorry, Ma'am. Tommy's dead."

The old lady, thinking that the event must have happened only a few minutes before, loudly gasped "Oh my god" and nearly fainted dead away.

With a glint in his eye, Sam mischievously then added, "But we have him packed in ice under the bus and we prop him up on the bandstand every night!"

"All you musicians are damned sickos" the old lady muttered loudly as she walked away.

♫

"Ghost bands" was a term often used by musicians referring to traveling bands where the original band-leader had passed away. To ensure that the band kept working, a replacement leader was hired by the family estate. Bands such as those of Genn Miller, Guy Lombardo, Count Basie, Tommy Dorsey, Artie Shaw, Jimmy Dorsey, Charlie Barnet, and Duke Ellington are prime examples.

♫

Las Vegas, despite its oppressive summer heat, had an magnetic appeal all its own. Work was plentiful for experienced musicians, and many eager players answered the call. As the continuing construction of

Boulder Dam in 1931 brought an influx of workers with a crying need for relaxation and cheap entertainment, night clubs and speakeasies such as The Red Rooster, Club Zanzibar, The Kit-Kat Klub, The Pioneer Club, The Igloo Club, The Camel Bar, The Meadows, and Frosty's Log Cabin sprang up with increasing regularity. Each new club brought with it a demand for bands and singers.

The often-heard term "floor show" came into being during this time. Since many clubs of the day had small dance floors but no permanent stage, bands often were placed at the side of the dance floor. When time came for the night's entertainment, an area was cleared away on the floor and the "floor show" commenced.

In backing the floor shows no special music for the bands was available at the time, so inexpensive printed music called "stock arrangements" were purchased in music stores.

♫

Not every plea for entertainment, though, was granted. At the nearby Boulder Dam construction site, when some of the musically oriented 5,000 workers asked the big bosses for permission to start a band for their own amusement, the loud emphatic answer was, "No way! We can't build no dam with no piccolo players!"

♪

Vegas became known as a real frontier town and western music was the style most appreciated. Groups with often humorous names such as Cactus Clint and his Prickly Pair, Butler's Nevada Riders, and The Rangemen found steady work along Fremont Street.

♪

Bass players of another genre were often the butt of many of Joe Venuti's more infamous practical jokes. Because he was such a world class jazzman and prominent stage personality, musicians eagerly answered the call to work gigs with the great Venuti.

On one memorable day in Hollywood, Joe called every bass player in the Los Angeles musicians' directory with a promise of work, and gave each instructions to meet him the next day at the corner of Hollywood and Vine Boulevards. As the appointed time arrived and one after another bass player showed up with his "axe" under his arm, invariably one or two would remark, "Hey man, are you on this gig too?" Soon, many dozens of tuxedo-clad perplexed bass players, with their instruments, milled about on the corner.

All the while, peering from a nearby hotel window, the irrepressible Joe Venuti sat watching as the whole scene unfolded. Even as the irate players filed charges with the union against him, Joe continued chuckling and gladly paid each a day's pay for the call.

♫

At an upper-class jazz club in Chicago, where Joe was appearing for several weeks, a perfect pay-back was given to Venuti by some fellow players.

Over 20 tuxedo-clad bass players, together with their large instruments, camped out on the doorstep of the jazz club waiting for Joe to arrive.

When, at last, he did appear, the smiling bass players held up a large sign with the words,

"Hey Joe, is this where the gig is?"

♫

Many hundreds of years before the birth of the four-mile-long street that came to be known as "the Vegas Strip," the first Native American people often came to the area now known as Tule Springs Park. (Tules in Spanish means reeds.) These Tule people, ancestors of modern-day Paiute/Shoshone tribes, undoubtedly brought with them members who were good story-tellers and drumbeaters.

Through the haze of a smoky campfire, you could almost hear a shaman say, "A funny thing happened on the way to the pow wow," followed by a loud drum roll on a hollow log.

The first musicians had at last come to the Las Vegas area!

"I don't know why I'm getting so fat! I only eat one meal a day. A salad and a cow!"
—Jack Sheldon, jazz trumpeter

As formative years of Las Vegas rolled by, there soon appeared on the "Strip" grand hotel casinos such as the beautiful El Rancho. As part of its welcoming customer-friendly atmosphere, the hotel, along with the necessary gaming, offered large musical productions for eager audiences.

One such show was a fairy tale sequence of Prokofiev's "Peter and the Wolf," complete with unique stage scenery, a company of scantily clad dancers and a large orchestra conducted by Ted FioRito.

The show progressed rather well until one night when near disaster struck. The lead trombone player, known to occasionally "sample the grape," had the all-important melody theme to play for "Peter" each time the actor appeared onstage. On that particular night he had sampled well beyond his share of the bottled grape and certainly felt no pain. When the dancer portraying Peter pranced onstage, the trombonist confidently played the solo theme on cue in perfect rhythm and intonation, but with one important thing missing----there not one correct note in the whole melody!

After finishing the solo, the bone player sat in his seat stiffly erect, looking straight ahead with no expression, and oblivious to events taking place in front of him.

Finally, after several interminably long minutes he leaned slightly toward to the trumpet player next to him and quietly whispered, "Was there any audience reaction?"

From that point on with the bandleader stunned, the lead dancer near collapse, other dancers giggling and the audience guffawing, the show was definitely on shaky ground!

"We've had lots of requests, but we're going to play anyway!"

—Ted Weems, bandleader

Many exciting events happen in Las Vegas showrooms, but not all are part of the plan.

Take for example this unexpected turn of events during an elegant show production at the El Rancho Hotel. With its large impressive scenery, the finely tuned Ted FioRito Orchestra, and a cast of showgirl/dancers beautifully costumed in heavy ballroom gowns, the show progressed rather nicely, until the unforeseen happened!

During one scene, as the newly hired showgirl/dancers spun, twirled and whirled to a waltz tempo around the stage, the heavily weighted ballroom gown of one dancer snagged part of the scenery.

In shocked disbelief, dancers watched as the lightweight scenery tumbled to the stage noisily, like falling dominoes, one into the next, and that into another until finally, the only things left visible to the stunned audience were a bright red fire extinguisher and a lighted "Exit" sign hanging on the backstage wall!

♫

During the mid-1950s the famous Shuffle Rhythm Orchestra of Henry "Hot Lips" Busse appeared for several nights at a National Undertakers' Convention in a famous Memphis landmark, the Peabody Hotel.

Formerly the featured trumpet player with the Paul Whiteman Symphonic Jazz Orchestra in the 1930s, Busse gained instant fame for his monumental hit recording of "Hot Lips" that swept the nation.

One night at the Peabody, as the orchestra was performing for the Undertakers' final banquet, Busse suffered a devastating heart attack that ended his life.

To finish up the band's contract at this important event, the Ted Weems Orchestra, appearing in another room downstairs, was quickly brought in as replacement.

Weems, with his usual dry caustic wit, was heard remarking to his own band,

"They're gonna have a helluva time getting a band for next year!"

♫

The luxurious Peabody Hotel, known worldwide for its beautiful accommodations and presentations of talent, was also known for greeting incoming guests in a rather unique way.

Happily placed every day in a gorgeous tile-lined fountain in the lobby, was a resident flock of noisy ducks, greatly enjoying being the center of attention of delighted guests.

After a busy day quacking and splashing in the pool, the birds at night time were then escorted to the elevator, often accompanying astonished fellow passengers of the human variety, as they took their nightly trip to pens on the rooftop of hotel.

♫

As men were drafted at the outbreak of WW II there was an immediate drain of personnel for bands. In an effort to keep their bands together, bandleaders of more than 200 name and semi-name bands volunteered their services for the war effort. One of the most famous of course, was the very large Glenn Miller Army Air Force Band.

To fill the need for musicians on the home front, "all girl bands" such as Phil Spitalny and his Hour of Charm Orchestra, Ina Ray Hutton and the Melodears, Dolly Dawn and the Dawn Patrol, and the International Sweethearts of Rhythm quickly came into nationwide prominence and did well their job of rallying the troops both at home and overseas!

CHAPTER TWO

GOOD THINGS STARTING TO HAPPEN

*"I could play higher, but my left
arm keeps giving out!"*
—Bitsy Mullins, lead trumpet Dunes Hotel

CHET ATKINS, famed multi-talented multi-instrumentalist guitar player, was walking one day along a busy street in Nashville when he came upon a young musician sitting on a doorstep playing his guitar. Stretched out in front of him was the ever present instrument case opened wide, hopefully awaiting donations from appreciative passersby.

Chet listened for several minutes and then commented, "That's a nice guitar you have there, son. Do you mind if I try it out?"

After being offered the guitar, Chet proceeded to play a blaze of chords, chromatic runs, and riffs with his usual amazing technique.

More than a little impressed, the younger player at last said, "You play pretty good, mister, but you ain't no Chet Atkins!"

♫

As the 1950's started to unfold, Vegas found itself awakening to the idea that this barren spot in the Mojave desert could possibly blossom into a major vacation destination spot for many entertainment hungry people.

With the late 1940s seeing at last the opening of the "Fabulous Flamingo Hotel Casino, " the brain-child of gangster Bugsey Siegal, other competitors sprang up quickly along the Strip. Although the Flamingo grand opening was a gigantic flop due to poor attendance, the first entertainers appearing in the showroom included Xavier Cugat and his band, Jimmy Durante, Rose Marie, and Georgie Jessel. Invited guests included such movie star idols as Clark Gable, Lana Turner, Judy Garland,

Robert Taylor, Van Heflin, Cesar Romero, Barbara Stanwyck, and Joan Crawford.

Hotel casinos such as the Tropicana, the Last Frontier, the Sahara, the Riviera, and the Hacienda, together with the magnetic appeal of gambling, offered entertainment of the likes never seen before. Every major hotel hired its own permanent "house-band" consisting of 12 or more musicians who remained solely at that hotel performing the music for each of the acts booked into the showroom. Major entertainment stars began appearing in showrooms along with their demands for excellent orchestras to back them.

Good things were definitely starting to happen in Vegas.

♫

On one occasion, a highly respected trombone player, a veteran of many nationally famous bands swooped into town to accept a job with bandleader Carlton Hayes' Desert Inn Orchestra. As was the usual routine, the player went to his first show at the hotel, played the first of two shows and then ambled across the street to the Silver Slipper Saloon, a favorite hangout for musicians between shows. One toast with old friends led to another and by the time he left for his second show at midnight, he was feeling no pain whatsoever. But instead of returning to the showroom where he was expected, he in his alcoholic glow went to the wrong hotel, climbed onto the bandstand, and sat down in the wrong bone section!

As the regular houseband filed in for the next show at midnight, the bone player looked around in utter amazement and exclaimed, "For christsake, I knew this cat fired lots of guys, but this is f***ing ridiculous!"

♫

In their continuing search for talent, hotel entertainment directors often hired many nationally known traveling bands whose names would fill their showrooms. Many popular large orchestras of the day, like those of Woody Herman, Benny Goodman, Tommy Dorsey, Jerry Gray, Jimmy Dorsey, Stan Kenton, Glenn Miller, Duke Ellington, Count Basie, Guy Lombardo, Jan Garber, Horace Heidt, Harry James, and others basked in the spotlight, adding much to the excitement and glamour of this "Tinsel Town" in the desert.

The Big Band era had arrived in Las Vegas.

♫

The El Rancho Vegas Hotel once featured the Charlie Barnet Orchestra in a series of blazing showroom concerts. Beldon Katleman, the hotel owner, apparently having no ear for artistic expression, one night turned off the stage lights and dropped the curtain in the midst of a smoking performance by the band.

It seemed that the show was running overtime and he didn't like the music!

"In music, everyone is a critic!"
—Duke Ellington, bandleader

Tommy Dorsey was well known for being a demanding person to work for, and while being such a perfectionist, when things sometimes went wrong, he usually found within the band a "whipping boy." It seemed that no matter however things happened or whoever made a mistake, Tommy would always rake over the coals veteran high note jazz trumpeter Charlie Shavers.

When asked by a buddy one night why he put up with all that abuse from Tommy for so many years,

Charlie answered: "It's mind over matter. I don't mind and HE don't matter!"

♫

At another time, the Dorsey band was performing on a live national TV show, along with Elvis in his first TV outing. During those early days before taped shows, the band was playing one of its featured numbers with the usual closeup camera work. As the "flag waver" neared its climax, the trumpet section stood up for the screaming "shout chorus." Everyone that is, except Charlie Shavers, who sat motionless in his seat, apparently fast asleep with two wide-awake eyes painted on his sunglasses!

Dorsey, on live camera yelled quite audibly: "SHIVERS, god damn it, get up!" Shavers leaped up, played some sizzling high notes at the end over the shouting band, and then took a big bow!

One of his fellow trumpeters asked him later "What note was it that you played on the end, Charlie?"

"What did it matter? It was high wasn't it?" answered Charlie.

♫

Joe Venuti, along with his amazing talent as a jazz violinist, possessed a wild man's sense of humor. During the late 1940s while working with a hot jazz band of the day, Joe had the opportunity to share the stage with a future Las Vegas resident, "Wingy" Manone, a Dixieland trumpeter of some renown. Manone, after losing his left arm in a childhood encounter with a trolley car, soon acquired his "Wingy" nickname along, with an artificial arm that proved to be no handicap to the trumpet man.

Venuti, in one of his devilish moods, would every year send Wingy on his birthday, a solitary cufflink!

♫

Heard at a band rehearsal, "Boys, I hear that we're coming back here next winter. The big boss just said it'll be a cold day when I hire that band again!"

♫

Bandleader Stan Kenton, always a stickler for his band members wearing correct uniforms onstage, would every night view with frustration the bare foot of jazz tenorman Zoot Sims.

It seemed that Zoot never wore the correct black socks and as a matter of fact, he wore none at all.

While sitting with the front row of saxophones, usually with his legs crossed, Zoot's lack of decorum was often very noticeable to the audience.

Finally, Kenton could stand it no longer. He quickly jumped up from the piano, grabbed Zoot's sockless foot, whipped out a bottle of black shoe polish, and proceeded to paint the tenorman's foot black!

♫

One witty trombone player remarked to his section mate, "When I retire, I think I'm going to move to a small town in Oregon, open a music store and then put a large mirror at the far end of the room so I can watch myself starve to death!"

♫

The music scene in Vegas began to come alive as one hotel followed another in presenting large spectacular shows with ever larger orchestras. Gone, happily, were the days when smaller sized show bands were the accepted rule. Musicians and bandleaders alike felt drawn to "this garden spot in the desert" with the prospect of work.

Showrooms that traditionally had been closed one night a week, found that staying open for the seventh night brought in added revenue. Since rules of the local musicians' union prevented players from working a full seven nights a week, there arrived on the scene a new form of orchestra called the "relief band," a completely different group that played the show on the houseband's regular night off.

♪

One such relief band, with a conductor barely adequate for the job, was accompanying a show at the Sahara Hotel showroom. Featured prominently during the show was a "line" of dancers who happily hoofed a complicated routine choreographed to last a comfortable twelve minutes.

On this particular night, though, the relief conductor deemed it exciting to speed up the tempos somewhat and proceeded to do just that. As a result, the twelve-minute line number was done in a frenetic sweaty, nine-minutes!

As breathless hard-working dancers ran back and forth into the wings of the stage one was heard muttering, "Let me at that little bastard. I'm gonna choke him!"

♪

Many bands have fine musicians who, like regular people happen to have stressful phobias of their own.

One such tenor player in the Dick Palombi Riviera Orchestra found himself with an uncontrollable, life-long fear of birds. Feeling that the fluttering of ruffled feathers along with their constant chirping made him nervous, the saxophonist shivered nightly as a featured Bird Act performed in the RIV showroom.

The act progressed rather well toward its usual finale with the star releasing a large white cockatoo to fly around the showroom. Amidst oohs and ahhs from the audience, the beautifully trained bird never failed to return to the trainer's waiting arm, but on one eventful night the bird performer had plans of its own!

With the band sitting in the orchestra pit at the side of the stage, the drummer played the usual loud drum roll and on cue the beautiful white bird dipped and swooped into the audience, gracefully circling the showroom not once but twice.

The full house of show-goers ducked and fear-fully shielded their heads from unwanted "bird-bombs" while the cockatoo, like a feathered dive bomber plummeted unerringly to the head of the sole person in the 2,000 seat showroom who most hated birds!

Instant chaos erupted in the orchestra pit as the large squawking bird with wings flapping mightily landed squarely on target! The fearful saxophonist loudly made his feelings well known while the band-leader chuckled and watched in amusement.

Luckily, despite frazzled nerves both bird and musician survived the resulting commotion and in true "show-biz" fashion, the show went on.

*"Never let your fingering interfere
with your playing!"*
—Bob Seidell, tenor man

Eager out-of-town gamblers with fat pocket-books were treated like VIP's by the big hotels. Planeloads of these convention "junkets" often were met at McCarran Airport and given the red carpet treatment by Dixieland bands and pretty showgirls. One enterprising singer was known to give an extra bonus to any cab driver who would strongly recommend and guide tourists to the showroom where he was appearing.

♫

"Show kids," as they called themselves, in Vegas production shows usually were hired for one of two distinct categories. They became either "show girls" or "dancers" and one job never blended into the other.

Slim and trim very fit dancers performed rigorous routines often demanded by drill instructor – style choreographers. Trained in ballet, swing and jazz, dancers never appeared topless in those shows sometimes labeled as "jiggle shows."

On the other hand, eye candy of the topless variety was performed by full-figured showgirls wearing elaborate feather covered costumes and not much else. Their job was to appear as semi-nude statues or, without dancing, to parade their charms around the stage.

Bandmembers in orchestra pits in front of the stage quickly memorized their music in order to appreciate the lovely passing scenery without the burden of reading music. It was one of those tough jobs expected, but they dutifully rose to the occasion!

Showrooms usually offered a "family show" with discreetly covered showgirls at eight o'clock while the "adult show" at midnight featured topless showgirls in all their glory.

Contrary to an often-heard rumor, major hotel showrooms never featured completely nude show-girls, although the coverings for certain strategic places was often the size of a large Band-Aid!

♫

It was always interesting to musicians that topless showgirls would go onstage strutting their stuff before an audience of thousands but when the show was over, band members often received scathing looks if they sneaked a peek!

♫

Vegas showbands, as a rule were very competent and played well the demanding music brought by entertainers. Since the music often had been recorded by nationally known big stars, it was expected that the bands perform the musical exactly as recorded.

Sometimes though, there arrived on the scene music that musicians quickly dubbed as "Oh Shit!" music.

As new music was being passed out at rehearsal for the next show, band members looking over their parts would sometimes remark, "There are a lot of notes here but it doesn't look too bad, does it?"

Then the conductor would count off the tempo

twice as fast as they expected and the exclamation "OHHH SHIT" was heard as they made a mad dash for their horns!

♫

Like the majority of entertainers appearing in Las Vegas, Tony Curtis was one of those acts that musicians enjoyed working. On one occasion at Caesars Palace, Tony was hired to be the Master of Ceremonies for a show that featured "Kids of the Stars." Such famous celebrities as Frank Sinatra, Mickey Rooney, Tony Martin, Cyd Charisse, and Gordon MacRae presented to the world their talented youngsters. In his job as MC, Tony was expected to introduce each of the performers, and he found plenty of free time at rehearsals to visit with the onstage Nat Brandwynne Orchestra.

Being a onetime amateur trumpet player himself, Tony loved to hang out with the trumpet section and during one of the rehearsals, one player mentioned that his all-time favorite film was "Some Like It Hot." Tony appeared with co-stars gorgeous Marilyn Monroe, Jack Lemmon and Joe E. Brown in that classic 1959 Billy Wilder movie.

Tony responded quickly by saying, " Oh really!, I have a copy of it in my car. I'll find a projectionist and we can watch it tomorrow night after the second show!"

He quickly hired a projectionist who remembered how to cope with the large number of 35mm film reels, catered a big buffet and invited all musicians, stagehands, stage carpenters, lighting men, entertainers on the show and whoever else who wanted to view the movie.

Later the next night, as the film was projected on the big dropdown screen, Tony went from table to table explaining how they had shot a particular scene and what fun it was for him to make that classic.

The hearty party went well into early morning and most certainly proved that Tony was one of the good guys!.

"Nothing improves your playing more
than being paid a salary!"
—Lester Young, Tenor man

Las Vegas had its own well thought-of recording studio often used by such top stars as Louis Armstrong and Julie London with Bobby Troup.

The major drawback to this quality studio was that it was located next to the Union Pacific railroad tracks. Whenever a freight train rumbled by, all recording was immediately shut down!

Despite that, some great recordings came out of those studios.

"There are just two kinds of music, the good kind and the other one!"

—Bitsy Mullins, lead trumpet Dunes Hotel

CHAPTER THREE

YOU ANIMAL, YOU!

*"Sometimes the trumpet wins, sometimes
you win. Tonight the trumpet won!"*
—Dizzy Gillespie, jazz trumpeter

EVERY SO OFTEN in a musician's career, he or she
may be accused of being "an animal" because of their
aggressive in-your-face way of playing. Bill Chase was
certainly considered an animal when playing lead
trumpet with Woody's band. Conrad Gozzo, Pete
Candoli, Wayne Bergeron, and Maynard Ferguson
were, without doubt, four trumpet playing "animals"

in the studio recording scene. When you add to this picture the real four legged, furry kind of animals that you sometimes encounter in your career as a professional musician, you have a interesting mix that may sometimes be fun, exciting and even dangerous.

Real animals can be unpredictable, and this is even more true when it involves a six-foot long boa constrictor. Consider this tale of Buddy Bair's small traveling territory band in Georgia and the act that they had to contend with.

As the orchestra arrived in their "sleeper bus" for a country club dance gig, Buddy, the bandleader was told that as part of the floor show that night they were to accompany an exotic dancer, "Wanda and her Trained Boa. " At the quick talk-through rehearsal, things went without a hitch and everything appeared to be fine and dandy. The star of the show, Wanda (sans her snakey companion) was seemingly content with the band.

Later that night on the show though, things rapidly went south as Wanda, in her slinky veils and cute little "asp," pranced onstage to do her part of the show. As the first notes of the music were played, the muscular snake coiling around Wanda suddenly tensed and started squeezing. No doubt he too was a music critic and didn't like the way his music was being played.

Naturally the band kept on playing, the boa constrictor kept on constricting and the dancer bravely struggled on with her act, although with each step a little more unsteadily. One of the trumpet players finally leaned over to his section mate and asked, "Is turning blue part of the act?"

At last after a few breathless, purple-hued moments, stagehands leaped into action and pulled the reluctant snake from around Wanda's bruised body. Both snake and Wanda were exhausted!

Quizzical band members were never quite sure exactly what the snake was supposed to do in the act or what Wanda would do for an encore!

♫

During the 1970s fat time for big bands in Vegas, there was a Donn Arden "production show" in one of the two MGM Hotel showrooms called "Hallelujah Hollywood." So-called production shows like this were really spectacular variety shows that included all sorts of different acts. Finding their 20 minutes of fame in the spotlight were jugglers, comedians, acrobats, animal acts, and elaborate dance routines often involving as many as 75 dancers, singers and large orchestras.

The trademark MGM lion, of movie logo fame

made his customary roar onstage at the opening of every show. Because of space limitations and no orchestra pit, the large Bill Costa Orchestra was placed in a room below stage with the music being piped into the showroom. Conductors and drummers followed the onstage action via closed circuit TV screens.

It so happened that the band room was situated next door to the very place where between shows, were kept the MGM lion and other assorted show animals. For every show, twice a night, the lion was taken to the stage area by his trainer. And, without fail, on every trip to the stage, the 800-pound lion would go to the closed band room door and "whizz" on it like a house cat marking his post. One whizz for every trip upstairs and another going downstairs for two shows every night presented a malodorous weekly total of twelve, plus a bonus two more for the third show on Saturday.

Naturally, the trainer tried to control the big kitty with his puny chain, but an 800-pound lion goes potty wherever he wants and his target seemed always to be the bandroom door! The door was repainted numerous times, "Cat-Begone" and "Cat-Scat" was sprayed on it, bleach was used and various other things tried with little effect. That big lion was one determined cat.

The show ran a record breaking seven years

with the MGM showroom presenting two shows a night, seven days a week, 12 months for every year. It amassed an amazing total of over 4,700 shows. That certainly was a lot of lion pee!

Gas masks and hazardous duty pay really should have been offered that band!

"Sure, jazz did come up the river to Chicago alright, but from MEXICO!"
—Luis Gasca, jazz trumpeter

Within its ranks, one showband produced a fine trombone player, who, despite having a heart valve replacement several years ago, found that his humor has never left him. He did admit though, that since the valve replacement was from a pig: "I can no longer eat bacon or pork because it might be a relative!"

Jazz, or "jass" as it was originally called was a New Orleans Creole word from the 1920s and was never spoken in polite society. The sexual connotation was considered too earthy for the delicate ears of most

N'Yawlins ladies. Old Dixieland tunes like "Jazz Me Blues" take on a new meaning in this context.

♫

Bandleader Ted Weems was a man who appeared to be as dignified and reserved as a bank president, yet who possessed a generally funny outlook on life.

During a road tour, the Weems band was appearing at a fashionable upscale country club gig in Oklahoma City when an admiring couple danced by the bandstand. In between tunes they engaged Weems in conversation. When they mentioned that they originally were from Boston, Ted replied, "Oh really, our drummer is from Boston." Turning to Jake Hanna, Ted said, "Jake, say something in Bostonese for these nice people."

"FAHT," said a smiling Jake!

"Don't change mouthpieces. Change gigs!"
—Wes Hensel, lead trumpet, Les Brown band

Not only famous for her "cookin' " gospel singers appearing at the Last Frontier Hotel, Clara Ward was also well known for her hot chili recipes that she loved to "whomp up" on any suitable occasion. Once, while trumpeter Roy Eldridge was in town with singer Ella Fitzgerald at the Flamingo Hotel, Clara and "Little Jazz" Roy cooked up enough chili to feed the small army of visiting musicians who dropped by for the all-day party at the motel.

Things progressed rather well during the afternoon until time came for both Roy and Clara to leave for their respective gigs. Completely forgotten on the stove was the large pot of red-hot chili still bubbling.

The pot boiled and bubbled and soon, as luck would have it, the room was also boiling and bubbling, resulting in a fire that turned the room to ashes and very nearly burned down the whole motel complex.

THAT was some hot chili!

"Hell is full of amateurs!"
—George Bernard Shaw, Irish playwright

When the popular Ted Weems Orchestra arrived for their latest dance gig at a fancy country club in Houston, they found that the club manager, unbeknownst to the bandleader, had made some plans quite unique for the night's festivities..

In the middle of their enormous swimming pool was a beautiful grand piano, (newly painted of course) perched precariously on a floating platform quietly awaiting the arrival of the band!

As the musicians, with much apprehension, started to load a small craft to take them to the platform, a slight breeze came up, rocking their little boat gently.

The gentle breeze soon turned into stronger gusts and tiny ripples in the pool became larger whitecaps until finally, with the stunned club manager watching in disbelief, his beautiful newly painted grand piano rolled back and forth across the tossing platform and soon made a large tsunami-like splash into the pool.

Under darkening skies, the 700-pound piano became an instant musical submarine that did not float too well, and the party mood was certainly dampened for the night.

♫

The New Frontier Hotel, following the Vegas trend for ever larger shows, soon came into its own with elaborate productions such as one entitled "Europa."

The rule of the day expected large orchestras, scantily clad dancers, singers with elaborate costumes, and, of course, the omnipresent circus acts with jugglers and animals.

Two separate animal acts of note in this production involved an opening act comedian/ventriloquist with his white duck, and another act having a trained tiger. Before being called on to do his part in the show, the big cat quite naturally was kept in a cage, and as stagehands stepped lightly, the overly friendly duck was allowed to stroll around backstage wherever it pleased.

As it often does with cats, curiosity can also get the best of ducks and one night as musicians were preparing their instruments for the upcoming show, one of the dancers came rushing into the bandroom exclaiming,

"OHHHH MY GOD, you won't believe this. The tiger has just eaten the opening act!"

♪

A jazz musician's view of today's music scene:

"Damn, the only people who like country western music is the public!"

A well-known percussionist in the Nat Brandwynne Caesars Palace Orchestra was quite notorious for being barely on time for every show. Despite several strong reminders from the bandleader to be onstage early, he would skate in at the last minute and in a darkened orchestra pit play a loud tympani roll announcing the beginning of the night's show.

One night though, a hilarious turn of events unfolded that left the bandleader fuming and band members red-faced with laughter.

As showtime loomed near, the breathless, always-nearly-late percussionist stepped confidently into the pit, picked up his mallets and produced his usual forceful roll on the tympani. The muffled un-musical sound erupting from the kettle drum was totally unexpected. The resulting noise was more like the thumping rumble of someone beating on a cardboard box!

The percussionist, in his usual breathless rush had forgotten to remove the customary cardboard coverings on the tympani heads!

♫

Like first chair violinists in a symphony, lead trumpet players are traditionally the concertmasters of big bands. At a rehearsal, one very experienced player was heard to proclaim to his section mates:

"This ain't no democracy, guys. It's MY way or the highway. It's A-440 or fight!"
—Bitsy Mullins, lead trumpet Dunes Hotel

At one hot Fourth of July concert, the Chicago Symphony was presenting its glorious rendition of Tchaikovsky's "1812 Overture" when a stunning turn of events made the concert one for the history books.

One of the French horn players, chosen not to play on this piece, was instead given a flashlight to be used as a signal. His flashed signal would cue the long row of Michigan Cannoneers when to shoot for the exciting grand finale.

As the orchestra, performing in its usual flawless style reached a midway point in the music, the musician, sitting high on his perch decided to make sure that the light would work well. He then proceeded to flash the beam several times to his satisfaction.

This signaled cue, although given accidentally in the completely wrong spot, was received by the waiting non-musical cannoneers, who, believing it to be grand finale time, eagerly touched off thunderous blasts from their long row of big guns.

The resulting ill-timed explosions nearly scared the wits out of both the unexpectant audience and orchestra alike, while covering everything with a dense smelly smoke. Somewhere lost in a gunpowder fog so thick that players could see neither music nor conductor, there poured forth quite a few interesting note combinations from the orchestra.

It was a concert certain to be talked about for years to come!

♫

Out of work musicians often take day jobs to tide them over until the next big gig comes along.

One sweet young pianist accepted a job as bank teller and in the process of doing her job one day, she waited on another Vegas musician.

Upon her being asked for help in balancing his checkbook, the young clerk responded nicely by saying, "Sir, I really am not supposed to do that for you. You have to do that yourself."

In a huff, the musician replied,

" I don't do math. You're the banker and I'm a musician. I'll bet you can't tell me the notes in a G7 chord"

She quickly answered, "Yes, I can. It's G-B-D-F natural, so balance your own damned checkbook!"

Bandleader Spike Jones often conducted his outrageous City Slickers Band with a toilet plunger.

CHAPTER FOUR

IT'S DEJA VU ALL OVER AGAIN

*"God so loved the world that he
gave us the trombone!"*
—Si Zentner, bandleader/ trombonist

NOT TOO MANY PEOPLE have ever heard of a
"chicken wire bandstand," in a club where the stage
was completely enclosed with heavy duty screen
wire and secured with a sturdy door that locked
on the inside. With the outside windows of the
bandstand also being screened, there usually was a
large slot in the door for passing drinks to the hard

working band. Many country western and Latin band musicians, on road tours through parts of the mid-west and south-west, soon found themselves facing bizarre bandstands such as this.

On one such gig, as the starting time approached, members of the Phoenix-based Pete Bugarin Orchestra were instructed to take their places onstage, to lock the bandstand door on the inside and to not come out for the duration of the dance. On seeing their quizzical expressions, the club owner, in a tone not too convincing, told them to "Just trust me, guys!"

The dance party progressed rather well, or so the bandleader thought, and as alcohol flowed generously each new tune found the crowd enthusiastically singing and dancing. Finally, at one point in the festivities after a mere two or three fights had been broken up, a UFO came flying through the air, smashing to bits against the bandstand screen accompanied by a deep voice growling,

"I told you not to play that god-damned tune!"

While band members ducked spinning shards of broken glass, the flying object was quickly identified as one being not very musician-friendly. Soon, more bottles hurtled through the smoky air and smashed onto the screen, no doubt echoing the original sentiments about the choice of tunes.

The fun time atmosphere was quickly restored and all soon forgotten with the playing of the next happy song.

The rest of the gig was fairly uneventful, and with frazzled nerves the band cautiously left the bandstand, tiptoeing out the back door into the night.

"The pen is mightier than the lip!"
— Ebbie Williams, lead trumpet Desert Inn Hotel

Shecky Greene, a very talented improvisational comedian and two-fisted drinker of renown, made a short jaunt one night up the street to another hotel to visit fellow comedians. As he swooped onto the long driveway lining the gorgeous fountains of newly opened Caesars Palace, he quickly neared the hotel entrance.

In his alcoholic glow, he made a hard right, and drove straight into the beautiful bubbling fountains!

While sitting calmly amidst all the swirling water and shouting of hotel security guards, Shecky slowly rolled down the car window and said: "NO SPRAY WAX"

♫

Jazz cornetist Bix Beiderbecke was a real freak for jello of any and all flavors. Once, while Bix did his thing on stage at a gig during one of those unusually cold Decembers of Chicago, a few of his buddies sneaked back to Bix's apartment, filled his bathtub with all the ingredients for making jello, and then opened the bathroom window letting in an icy blast.

The resulting concoction surprised and thrilled Bix to no end!

♫

Bandleader Ted Weems, responding to a request by a dancing couple, "Sorry, folks we don't have that tune in our book, but this next one has a lot of the same notes in it!"

♫

A mobster boss, surrounded by his big body guards with even bigger guns, strolled into a Vegas piano bar and sat in a corner booth. Finally, as the pianist, trying not to rile anyone's temper, played quietly, one of the bent-nose cauliflower-ear type hoods walked over, threw a $20 bill in the tip jar and said in a gruff voice, "Da big boss ova dere wants you should play a tune for 'im, "Come Rain or Come Shine." Either one!"

♫

During one never to be forgotten performance at Caesars Palace, famed pianist/comedian Victor Borge watched helplessly as the relief orchestra, hampered by a less than competent conductor, struggled mightily. When at last the show had reached its all-time low point, Victor could stand it no longer. He walked over to the orchestra pit, stopped the music and leaning down asked the bandleader: "Excuse me sir, what exactly do you do here?"

"I'm the conductor," answered the trembling bandleader.

"In that case, give me a transfer!" said Borge as he stomped away.

♫

As the sweet young vocalist arrives at the rehearsal being held especially for her, the bandleader says: "We have a new chart for you. You'll sing the first three bars in the key of C, then you'll modulate up a half-step for two and a half bars and then down a whole step. One measure is in 4/4, the second in 3/4 and the third is in 5/4 time."

"Wait a minute, are you crazy?" she exclaims. "I can't sing a tune like that!"

"Why not, you did last night!" answered the disgusted leader.

♫

As Woody Herman's hot band was performing on a "live" TV show one summer evening with famed singer Sarah Vaughan, an interesting turn of events occurred that almost stopped the show.

Originating from WGN Chicago the programmed show lineup was to feature Woody's clarinet and the "Fourth Herd" on several swinging tunes, then followed by the spot to showcase the dynamic star of the show, "Sassy" Sarah Vaughan, with some of her hit tunes. One of the planned songs was Sarah's international big hit of the day, "Misty," the theme song from the current movie "Play Misty for Me."

At rehearsal things went well with the band at the ready, all lighting, sound equipment and scenery in place and a nice show expected. Along with the band being placed onstage behind a decorative screen, there also were several large tubs to be filled later with boiling water. When stagehands at the appointed time dropped large chunks of dry ice into the tubs, thick smokey clouds of "mist" would billow up, setting the mood perfectly for Sarah's rendition of her hit song.

At the well organized rehearsal, the stagehands were told that Sarah would sing THREE tunes, the last one being "Misty," and with that information filed away mentally, they wandered off to relax a bit before the show.

During the live show though, with no one advising the stagehands of the change, another tune was added to the program lineup and "Misty" became the FOURTH tune to be sung.. As Sarah sang her third tune, the unaware stagehands had counted "1st, 2nd, 3rd tunes, it's time" and dumped pounds of dry ice into the hot water. The resulting billows of mist swirled up enveloping Sarah in a dense fog bank, while she bravely continued singing a completely different ballad, something like "On The Sunny Side of the Street!"

The stagehands vainly tried, with no success to sweep back the fog and when the time came for Sassy Sarah to actually sing "Misty" in its proper spot, there was no dry ice mist to be had.

Ahhh, such are plans well laid on live TV.

♫

A young bystander asked a featured trombone soloist after a concert:

"Where does that slide go anyway?"
—Glenn Shull, Colorado trombonist

In the not-so distant past of the 1960s, many African-American performers were not allowed to stay
in the multi-million dollar Vegas hotels where they
appeared. Such stars as Sammy Davis, Jr., Ella Fitzgerald, and Nat King Cole, and their musicians often
were made to enter the hotel showrooms through
the kitchen. Traveling Black accompanists of stars
usually found lodging next door to the Flamingo
Hotel at The Cromwell Motel, the present site today
of the Barbary Coast Hotel. The unbending rule was
that Black performers could stay there but under no
circumstances were they allowed to swim in the pool.

On one occasion when Ella's musicians, jazz
guitarist/flautist Les Spann, drummer Gus Johnson,
and trumpeter "Little Jazz" Roy Eldrige checked
into the motel, a quick phone call from the office
confirmed that the pool was a definite no-no.

Later that afternoon at the rehearsal for Ella's
upcoming show, as her musicians related their story

to Russ Black's Flamingo Band, the local players quickly schemed on a plan to remedy the situation.

On the very next day, in bright sunny daylight, the entire Flamingo band, along with Ella's musicians, Roy, Les and Gus, jumped into the Cromwell Motel pool in front of Las Vegas, God, and the whole world and had a raucous good time swimming to their hearts' content!.

From then on, the pool was cool!

♫

Another of Venuti's seemingly endless practical jokes occurred during a long road trip through the southwest. Involving a bass player with whom he was not overly fond, Joe concocted a fiendish prank that succeeded in tormenting his hapless victim. At any opportunity, in finding the bass left unguarded, Joe would secretly pour a cup full of sand, from nearby cigarette ashtrays, into the F-holes of the instrument. Soon, as one night stretched into another, not only did the bass become increasingly heavier, but the sound became more dull.

After several weeks, the perplexed bassist was duly convinced that was "losing his chops," and that he must have been struck by some debilitating road malady!

♫

Overheard at rehearsal were instructions being given to the band by a well known relief band leader in the 1970's: "When you get to the ritard at the end, just ignore it and slow down a little bit!"

♫

Every band seems to have a player who, all by himself, lives life right on the hairy edge. One such notable character was a trombonist in the Ray Sinatra Tropicana "Folies Bergere" Orchestra.

Herein lies the tale.

Always flirting with being late for the downbeat, as showtime neared one night the bone player found the usual entry to the orchestra pit closed and he made a mad dash through the stage curtain to the pit area.

Waiting expectantly in front of the curtain, stood a lovely showgirl, beautifully arrayed in feathers and sequins, ever at the ready to do her spiel announcing the beginning of the show.

The musician, in his breathless scramble to get to the pit before the downbeat, stepped through the curtain and right in front of the showgirl EXACTLY at the moment the pin spotlight flashed on for her show announcement.

There in the bright spotlight, transfixed like a deer in the headlights, stood the trombonist frozen in time with his instrument in one hand and his usual glass of sipping water in the other!

As he jumped down into the pit landing noisily, the red-faced bandleader blurted out some choice words and gave the "evil-eye" to the bone player for rest of the night.

♫

Performing shows, needless to say, sometimes can be more than a little exciting and nerve-wracking for musicians.

Take for example this event that occurred one night with the Ray Sinatra Orchestra while performing the Tropicana "Folies Bergere" show.

As the band played a rousing rendition of Katchturian's "Sabre Dance," the trio of "Kuban Cossacks," costumed like traditional old time Russian soldiers, wildly dashed around the stage with exciting sword twirling acrobatics.

The finale quickly came to its climax with the sharply pointed military weapons being tossed in the air round and round, backwards and forwards to each of the dancers.

Somehow, one of the dancers missed catching his

sword and like a spear it unerringly streaked into the orchestra pit, impaling itself in the wall inches away from the stunned upright bass player!

Without having to think twice, the pale-faced bassist decided to sit out the next tune and made a hasty retreat to the nearest bathroom!

♫

Two saxophonists from the Riviera Orchestra, on their way home one night at the finish of their last show, spotted a jogger trotting easily along in the cool evening.

"Watch this," said the practical joker-driver to his friend as he pulled alongside the runner.

Continuing to move along beside the jogger, he asked with a big friendly smile, "Pardon me, sir. Can you give me directions to 1500 South Las Vegas Boulevard?"

"Sure," answered the helpful runner. "Go two blocks to the right and then ten blocks to the left. You can't miss it."

While at the same time asking more questions, the musician was gradually increasing his car speed and the jogger, without realizing it, tried vainly to keep up!

Finally, after a few exhausting blocks, the breathless runner came close to breaking Roger Bannister's record for the four minute mile and he at last gave up the chase!

Chuckling heartily, the musician then sped away into the night leaving a red-faced runner gasping for air at the side of the street!

"Flamenco dancers look like a bunch of guys trying to put out a grass fire!"
—Bob Seidell, saxophonist

CHAPTER FIVE

HANG ON 'ROUND THE TURNS

"I've gotta get out of Vegas. This town's driving me crazy. Last night in my neighborhood alone we had THREE DRIVE-BY TRUMPET SOLOS!
—Carl Fontana, jazz trombonist

ETHEL MERMAN, that very popular star of the 1960s, with the strongest lungs of all Broadway, planned in great detail the highly publicized grand opening of her new show at the Flamingo Hotel in Vegas.

With a large cast of dancers, backup singers, and

fresh new arrangements for the Russ Black Orchestra, the costly production promised to be a real treat for friends and critics alike. A huge number of Invitations were doled out to show reviewers of major magazines, innumerable press photographers, and many movie star friends from Hollywood, promising the full house most certainly an exciting opening night.

Because of space limitations and the large cast, the orchestra was placed in a crowded pit area directly in front of the stage. Almost touching the elaborate old style stage curtain with its many tassels, folds and rope chains stood the orchestra bass player with his upright instrument, in anticipation of the downbeat for the beginning of the show.

Following a loud timpani roll from the percussionist, came the announcer's booming voice: "Ladies and gentlemen, the Fabulous Flamingo Hotel proudly presents Broadway star, Miss Ethel Merman!"

With Merman waiting nervously in the wings of the stage, and the audience sitting quietly in breathless anticipation of an outstanding performance, the stage curtain began going up.

The stunned bandleader watched in horror as the bass player's instrument, with its tuning pegs hopelessly entangled in the ruffles and swag of the curtain material, began rising to the high ceiling along with the curtain.

The bass player, finding himself being pulled relentlessly upward at an alarming rate, desperately held on to his prized instrument refusing to let go. Finally, amidst screams from the audience and shouts from the band, another musician close by grabbed and hung onto his dangling legs, yelling to him,

"Turn loose, man! "

"Hell no," was the answer "this is my favorite bass! "

Throughout the long history of show biz, there never was a "show stopper" quite like this one!

♫

It seems that every showband had at least one practical joker and sometimes more than one.

One well thought of trumpet player in Al Alvarez's New Frontier Band, who happened to be a notorious practical joker himself, would go onstage every night at showtime with a jug of water to wet his whistle as he played the show. Having a chronic dry mouth while playing, he would often sip a little water poured from an opaque fruit juice container beneath his music stand.

On one hot summer night as the show neared its end, the trumpet player reached for one last sip of water from the jug. As he tilted the pitcher to get that last drop of H2O from it, he heard a strange flapping sound coming from within.

Other bandmembers watched gleefully as a bright shiny goldfish plopped noisily into his cup!

♫

Another Kodak moment with Joe Venuti in the late 1920s happened as the great jazz violinist traveled with Paul Whiteman's Symphonic Jazz Orchestra. Oftentimes, as near terminal boredom set in, practical jokes flew like a flock of birds on the bandstand.

Each night, like clockwork, the portly conductor would arrive at the gig impeccably dressed in a white suit, white shirt with black tie, white shoes, and his ever present derby hat, which he hung precisely in the same spot as the night before.

Not being one to pass up an opportunity like this, Venuti soon had devised a devilish plan to drive Whiteman wild.

Earlier in the day, Joe had purchased six derby hats, identical to Whiteman's, except for one small detail. Each derby was in a progressively smaller size. Every night for a week, Joe waited for the right moment and furtively replaced the leader's derby with one of a smaller size.

By the end of the week, the hypochondriac Whiteman became more and more convinced that he had contracted some terrible disease that made his head swell more everyday!

*"If we had to eat the music we
listen to, we'd all die!"*
—Bandleader Artie Shaw in an interview
with author Bill Clancy

One of the fine violinists who worked in most of the major string sections around Las Vegas had fun stories to tell of his pre-professional music years.

Always being fascinated with the idea of flying, he as a kid in the late 1920s, used to hang around the airfields near his small hometown in Utah. Most of the fragile planes in those days shortly after WWI were of the bi-plane variety, having two cloth covered wings held together by struts and wire cables.

It so happened that the mechanics at the field, where the budding musician hung out everyday, seemed never to be able to correctly adjust the wire cables necessary for proper tension between the wings. Improper tension, of course, meant sagging wings which translated into disaster for the pilot.

Having a trained ear, the young musician was put to good use when he landed a job "tuning" the wing cables just like a violin string. When all cables reached the same pitch by his twisting of the turnbuckles, wing tension was correct and the plane airsafe.

In exchange for performing this daily chore, he got the thrill of his young life with free rides in the planes and some flying lessons thrown in for good measure. One sunny day though, brought with it events that became a little more exciting than he had hoped for.

On this eagerly awaited day, while taking a few free lessons, he found himself in the front cockpit of an open two-seater "Jenny" bi-plane. The friendly instructor was, as usual actually flying the plane from the backseat, and things were going along well as the young musician enjoyed himself immensely.

After being aloft for a short while, he heard singing and laughing, although the plane had no radio, and as he turned to see where the noise was coming from, the boy got one of those "OH SHIT!" sensations in his throat!

The instructor, like a cowboy riding a bull, was out of the cockpit astride the fuselage of the plane, screaming "Yahoo" like a banshee and waving an empty bottle of booze in the thin air. So, here was the wide eyed teenager at 5,000 feet over Utah in a plane that as yet, he could neither fly nor land, along with a loaded instructor who could possibly fall off at any minute.

Although sounding like the plot of an old-fashioned horror movie, this particular violin player has since gone on to become a much sought-after professional in Las Vegas string sections. Obviously, the young musician, somehow, was able to convince the inebriated pilot that falling off was not such a good idea and climbing back in the cockpit to land it was a much better choice.

"I can't listen to that much Wagner. I start getting the urge to conquer Poland!"
—Woody Allen, comedian

The innovative Stardust Hotel Lounge had a rather unique stage setup for its time, a revolving circular bandstand. With the large round stage divided by a curtain down the middle from side to side, as one act was performing its show for the audience, the next act was getting ready behind the screen.

When the first act was playing its last notes, the stage would begin revolving slowly, and the next act would magically appear playing their opening tune. It was a remarkable visual transition with sometimes an interesting blend of music.

Along with many diverse acts like the Kim Sisters, the Harmonicats, and the exciting recording orchestra of Esquivel, featuring high note jazz trumpeter Louis Valizan, the lounge lineup promised fine entertainment for an evening.

"There are just three registers in playing trumpet. The high register. The low register. And the CASH REGISTER!"
—Clark Terry, jazz trumpeter

For its grand opening, the Tally Ho Hotel, a short lived but innovative gambling-free, smoke-free establishment presented in its showroom a mini-production that included dancers, singers, topless show-girls, the small but mighty Brian Farnon's 8-piece Band, and a featured dance routine labeled as an "Adagio Act."

A beautifully choreographed adagio act includes a petite semi-nude female dancer being held aloft during the performance by the strong hands of her muscular male partner. With beautiful stage lighting, accompanied by soft languid music from the orchestra, the mood is set for a sensual scene.

During the entire 4-5 minute performance, the nude 100-pound "girl" dancer never touches the floor as her buff partner skillfully changes positions in time with the music. Never failing to wow the audience, her beautiful movements contrasting with the strength of his body, makes for a truly lovely scene.

On the hotel's opening night, with five one-hour shows scheduled beginning at midnight, the first and second went beautifully. The petite girl was lifted smoothly as her supremely confident partner completed his moves with ease. Show producers and dancers alike were all smiles as the final curtain ended the first two shows.

The third show, though, quickly presented a few problems, and as the male dancer started to struggle somewhat to continue, he felt his strength starting to slip away. Held aloft on his upraised hand, the nude girl smiled beautifully and gracefully completed her moves, but the couple sensed problems in the making. There was an obvious need to eliminate several classic moves in the show.

At the opening curtain of the fourth show, the night took a turn for the worse, and things started going south rapidly. As their routine progressed, her supporting partner tried mightily, but with the excitement and frazzled nerves of opening night, found his strength completely gone. No matter how much he tried, he found it impossible to lift the petite 100-pound topless girl over waist high.

As the band repeated the same music phrases over and over in a "vamp," members eyed the stage expectantly and to a man everyone there mentally tried to encourage the struggling dancer onstage.

In desperation, in order to keep the momentum going for the act, the girl dancer vainly tried taking a few flying leaps into the waiting arms of her profusely sweating partner. His sweaty palms and her slippery body made it apparent that now was the time to tactfully exit stage-right!

Taking quick bows on a quickly dimming stage, the couple left to lick their wounds and plan for another day.

Because of lack of strength and lack of interest from the audience, as the sun came up the fifth show was mercifully cancelled.

♫

Animal acts are sometimes found to be mistreated by their trainers backstage (before PETA becomes aware) and it usually gives musicians great pleasure when animals like these get an opportunity to give back some of that abuse.

Take for example this, a sea lion act performing at the Riviera Hotel main showroom involving a huge 800-pound bull sea lion and a 120-pound trainer, who later proved to be very abusive to his animals.

The finale of his act came with thunderous applause from the audience as the muscular trainer did an impressive one-armed handstand on the nose of the big sea lion. One night though, after months of suffering, the sea lion apparently decided that enough was enough and tonight would be payback time!

While the drummer played a loud timpani roll and the trainer attempted to do his usual crowd pleasing stunt, the audience held its collective breath as the animal tensed his huge neck muscles. With the slightest twist of his neck, the sea lion flipped the surprised trainer 15 feet into the audience atop a table, and then streaked offstage to his open cage!

Although the sea lion must have paid dearly for his little bit of revenge, the band, to a man thought: "Good for the sea lion!"

♫

A guitarist member of the TCB band on tour with Elvis doing his usual full schedule of shows, relates how the enthusiastic screaming girls in the audience sometimes would drown out signals to the band.

"Since we often could not hear the signals, we would have to watch the body movements of Elvis to get a clue what to play next.

The "Taking Care of Business Band" was the only band I had ever heard of that was directed by an ASS!"

♫

One night at the Tropicana Hotel's long running "Folies Bergere" show, a mischievous percussionist thought it would be fun to play a prank on the unsuspecting dancers in the cast.

Going into the orchestra pit 15 minutes earlier than actual showtime, he proceeded to play a loud timpani roll, just like the one he would usually play to announce the beginning of the show.

Absolute pandemonium exploded backstage as

25 half-dressed dancers scrambled from dressing rooms and down noisy metal stairs screaming and cursing mightily: "OH MY GOD, what is that idiot doing. He's fifteen minutes early!"

The curtain finally went up with the entire red-faced cast zipping up costumes, tucking things in here and there, while glaring daggers at the drummer!

♫

Drummer/band leader Buddy Rich, lying on a gurney on his way to surgery was asked by a doctor,

"Are you allergic to anything?"

"Yeah, country western music!" he answered!

CHAPTER SIX

HOW SWEET IT WAS

"Stick around after the show for the big fight,
folks. They're not going to pay the band!"
—Shecky Greene, comedian

A VETERAN LEAD TRUMPETER in Vegas who was a member of one of Benny Goodman's precision bands relates the tale of a humorous incident that happened during a concert.

During a program featuring the band and a down-home blues guest singer, a very large woman with an equally impressive Afro hairdo, a comical turn of events almost destroyed the band with laughter!

The agreed upon program for the concert was that when she finished her choruses, the singer would take her bows and exit to the left, while at the same time, Benny would enter from the other side for his turn at the microphone.

At the appointed time, Benny, always like an absent-minded professor, wandered in on the WRONG side. As the singer finished her tunes, took a low sweeping bow and made a hard left to exit the stage, Benny, in his constant fog, swung his clarinet up to play, hopelessly entangling the keys in her luxurious hairdo!

She pulled and he pulled and as the curly hair/clarinet key tug-of-war unfolded at the microphone, the snickering band bravely tried to continue playing.

Finally disentangled after 24 measures of squeaking and squawking, along with the careful removal of long, curly hair from clarinet keys, "the King of Swing" completed his choruses, smiling broadly as if nothing had happened!

♫

Bandleader, overheard on bandstand at rehearsal asking guitar player, "Why are you taking so long to tune up? Segovia takes only a few minutes."

To which the miffed guitarist answered, "Maybe Segovia didn't care!"

♫

On another occasion came proof that by design musicians are creatures of habit.

The bus for Les Brown's "Band of Renown" was late getting to the gig, leaving no time for supper and with everyone scrambling to change clothes. One trumpet player, who happened to be diabetic, stopped by the club bar for a glass of orange juice to take with him on the bandstand.

As the night progressed, the trumpet player, feeling himself starting to slip into low blood sugar from lack of food, reached down for a sip of orange juice just at the exact time when he was supposed to play a jazz chorus.

As the expected spotlight beamed brightly on him, he realized foggily that he should be doing something at that time in the music, so he stood up and drank his orange juice for eight bars!

*"Why do lute players spend half the
time tuning up, and the other
half playing out of tune?"*
— Victor Borge, pianist/ comedian

In the later months of 1969, the grand opening
of Kirk Kerkorian's mega-resort International Hotel
(later the Las Vegas Hilton) dazzled the city with the
elegant first-time appearance of Barbra Streisand in
the main showroom.

While Peggy Lee and a large orchestra held forth
in one of the hotel's large lounges, Elvis Presley
began his big comeback with a complete media blitz
and a spectacular show. Beautifully crafted arrangements of his favorite tunes were done for the large Joe
Guercio Orchestra, which included a string section,
a vocal backup group and Elvis' usual "Taking Care
of Business" rhythm section.

Lean and trim, dressed in a blazing white jump-
suit, Elvis performed energetically for excited fans
at every show. Age was no barrier for the audiences
as "Elvis The Pelvis" thrilled the crowds young and
old, with familiar yet still vibrant versions of his hits.

As a sidebar, the International Hotel showroom seated 2,000 guests per show, twice a night, seven days a week for an entire month, making an impressive total of 120,000 eager fans of all ages. This sold out Elvis event occurred three times a year with never an empty seat!

♫

Although Elvis' many adoring fans and his ever-growing popularity made him a near-prisoner in his hotel penthouse, he found several ways to entertain himself in the off-hours. As he was unable to attend public places such as hotel swimming pools and restaurants like everyday Dick and Jane, he became fascinated with guns and practiced constantly with a pair of six-shooters loaded with real bullets! Often standing before full length mirrors, he pictured himself being a fast-draw gunslinger like one of the Old West cowboy bad guys.

As he practiced his gun technique every day, Elvis usually would watch three different television shows at the same time, but he developed a unique way of changing channels. When a program came up that he didn't like, he would fast draw his loaded pistol and shoot out the TV screen!

A quick call to the front desk was usually met with

a tired sigh and the muttered words, "Somebody take another television up to Elvis! He's done it again!"

♫

On the road with the Johnny Long Orchestra, the band bus came over a hill, and in seeing a long line of cars going in the same direction, the bandleader confidently told the driver to follow those cars up ahead: "I'm sure they're going right to our gig at the ballroom."

After a few more minutes of following along, the bus came over another hill and they watched in amazement as the long line of cars turned into the entrance for a drive-in movie!

♫

The Desert Inn Hotel, in keeping up with its Strip competitors, produced large elegant shows of its own, each one more exciting than the last.

One such show, including the large Carlton Hayes Desert Inn Orchestra, plus an equally big company of dancers, showgirls, and singers was made up of a few old-fashioned nostalgic scenes like the following:

As part of a scene featuring one of the favorite songs from the early 1900's, "On Moonlight Bay," a bright yellow crescent moon suspended by cables would drop down from the very high backstage ceiling. Two singing lovers, sitting on the moon prop called a "fly away," would then render their featured number and when finished, the moon, along with the two singers, would then be pulled up out of sight for the necessary quick change of scenery.

As the scene ended with the dropping of the front screen, the fly-away moon would then come down, depositing the singers safely on firm ground. At least that was the expected plan.

One night, though, as the last notes of the finale were being sounded, the stage manager asked if anyone had seen "Joe and Sallie," the two singers from the moon scene. They were nowhere to be found.

After much calling out and searching with no luck, finally someone looked up into the loft and there sat the two singers, 25 feet above the stage hoarsely yelling for help!

Stagehands had somehow forgotten to lower the "fly-away" moon at the end of the scene, and the singers, with white knuckles and pink faces, had hung on desperately for a half hour, waiting for the end of the show.

"Jazz is the thinking man's music!"
—Art Blakey, drummer/bandleader,
The Jazz Messengers

The late '60s and early '70s proved to be exciting times for musicians in "Tinsel Town," as more beautifully designed hotel resorts opened with much fanfare.

With a grand opening at the magnificent new Caesars Palace Hotel that outshone all others, no expense was spared.

In the main showroom featuring singer Andy Williams, ably accompanied by the 48-piece Nat Brandwynne Orchestra and ten backup singers, there was an elaborate 15-minute opening production number called "Rome Swings." With its well-rehearsed company of dancers, showgirls and singers all dressed scantily in mini-togas, the line number was an immediate hit with eager audiences.

Throughout the casino, tucked here and there in random lounges, were several single pianists or piano and bass duos, plus in the king-sized 24-hour show lounge were featured acts such as Della Reese,

Mary and the Maoris, and Eartha Kitt. Oftentimes, as many as two 15-piece bands accompanying acts were busily working there.

A large floating "Cleopatra's Barge" featured a varied number of salsa and rock bands that drew big numbers of the younger crowd into its bar area. With exciting music from over 100 musicians working year-round throughout the hotel, large crowds responded happily.

At the Sands Hotel, the newly redesigned Sands Hotel showroom featured nightly such popular stars as Frank Sinatra, Sammy Davis Jr., Dean Martin, Shirley MacLaine, and Joey Bishop along with the fine Antonio Morelli Orchestra. Often appearing individually, this group later would become known as the Rat Pack, and large crowds attended just to see how outrageous the unscripted show would become!

♫

At a long, tedious show rehearsal, one sideman finally asked the bandleader, "Boss, we've been on the bandstand for two hours now. Don't you think it's time to give us a bathroom break?"

The leader quickly answered,

"Now, guys, you've known about this gig for months now!"

♬

Some musicians were known to supplement the income of their music gigs by also working daytime jobs. In blistering hot Vegas weather, these outdoor jobs understandably were often tiring and exhausting.

Take for example this story of the houseband piano player during a mainroom show at the Riviera.

The show at the time, featured, among others, a ventriloquist with his assortment of character dolls, and as customary part of his act, the star would bring a chair to sit at the edge of the stage close to the orchestra as he performed a quiet routine. To accompany him, the pianist sitting in the darkened pit would play soft background music presenting a perfect setting for a nice, intimate scene.

One night, though, sounding as if someone were playing with his knuckles, strange un-musical notes came clunking and banging from the piano!

As the rest of the quiet band came out of its fog and looked around, the ventriloquist stopped his act, peered into the pit and said, "What the f*** is going on down there?"

It seems that the pianist, after an exhausting day working at his construction job outdoors in super-hot weather, had dozed off while playing the usual quiet accompaniment. Being a creature of habit like most musicians, he realized he should be doing something at that moment, so he kept his hands moving at the piano with some interesting results.

"Bill Berry didn't fire me from his band. He just stopped telling me where the gigs were!"

—Jack Sheldon, Jazz trumpeter

CHAPTER SEVEN

FULL CONTACT MUSIC

*"Saddle up, boys. We'll cut
'em off at the pass!"*
—Carlton "Hap" Hayes, bandleader Dunes Hotel

WITH ANOTHER of his endless practical jokes, a mischievous Joe Venuti tormented his fellow bandmate, jazz trumpeter Wingy Manone on yet another occasion.

While rooming in NYC, the duo drove each night to their four-week-long jazz gig in a club near the city. On every night for a entire month, Joe would give

Wingy precise instructions as to how to get to the gig:

"It will take us about an hour, so first go through the Holland Tunnel, then head twenty miles south, turn right for fifteen miles, then make a turn heading north for thirty miles and we'll be right at the club."

But, on the very last day of the month-long gig, Joe told Wingy that if he didn't mind he would prefer to drive that night.

And getting in the car Joe then gleefully drove a brief FIFTEEN minute trip to the gig!

♫

A comment quietly heard at a concert:

"See that guy over there? He always wanted to play bassoon in the worst way, and he does!"
—Sam Pisciotta, lead alto saxophonist

During the first months of its grand opening, the colorful Circus Circus Hotel featured two 15-piece bands, dressed in colorful circus uniforms, to accompany acts usually seen in a circus. With each group working six-hour sets, the bands backed a dozen different acts of every sort imaginable. Acts with small dogs jumping through hoops and chimps dancing filled the stage while high flying acrobats ruled the swings up above. There were twelve continuous hours of musically accompanied circus acts!

♫

In the compact main showroom of Circus Circus, at the same time of its grand opening, there also appeared a mini-production show with an Old West theme. Along with its sparse saloon scenery, a medium sized cast in vests and cowboy boots, plus the 12-piece R.V. Brand Orchestra, the mini-show received good reviews and drew nice crowds.

With the show producer himself being a movie stuntman, the Old West themed show featured a scene with two actual Hollywood stuntmen with knives and bullwhips, who would carefully act out a bar room fight. In the scene, as one bad guy cowboy, brandishing a bolo knife threatened the other, the second would return the favor with the stinging lash of a 9-foot long leather bullwhip.

One night, though, at backstage, the two stuntmen apparently had a slight disagreement that continued onstage and escalated with every show afterwards. Pointed knife jabs and bullwhip lashings became more intense with each show.

Finally, one much abused cowboy could stand the

whip no longer, and as he made a flying leap at the other, there began a real life non-scripted brawl on stage. With fists flying, much yelling and Styrofoam scenery everywhere crashing to the floor, the entire stage became an arena for the two tussling stuntmen.

Meanwhile, with the audience watching in open mouthed disbelief, the band, as usual, kept playing and playing and playing.

Finally, the battle came to an end as the stunt-man/producer, who happened to be in the audience that night, jumped onstage and pulled apart the two combatants.

The short run of the show had ended with a real bang!

"A band should have a sound all its own, a real personality."
—Glenn Miller, bandleader

The entertainment director of Circus Circus, always trying to dream up something unique to attract audiences, came up with an outrageous stunt for two trombone players from the circus band.

He asked them to play, while hanging by the ankles UPSIDE DOWN and suspended by a moving track in the high ceiling! One complete circuit of the track around the casino area would last a blood rushing ten minutes.

Fortunately, that crazy idea soon fizzled because of a definite lack of interest shown by the fearful musicians. Being suspended upside down while playing thirty feet above the casino floor was not exactly a dream job sought after by many.

After tossing the original idea aside, another one more reasonable replaced it. Scantily clad showgirls wearing big smiles and little else, sitting astride carousel horses moving along the ceiling track, tossed out colorful balloons to tourist/gamblers below.

♫

The Riviera Hotel's beautiful show lounge often featured two different acts per night, such as singer Vic Damone and comedian Shecky Greene, each with his own 15-piece band. Because of its wide variety of entertainment, the lounge did amazing business, but for some unexplained reason, it was doomed by the hotel bosses to become another 24-hour Keno room, totally without music.

On the closing night of this popular musician-friendly show lounge, Shecky Greene's pianist/ conductor Herbie Dell and the big band of Carl Lodico watched in amazement as Shecky, like someone possessed, grabbed a fireman's axe from the backstage wall and proceeded, with a vengeance, to chop up center stage!

As he hacked away, Shecky then passed small souvenir pieces of the stage to the audience.

♫

Composer/singer/pianist Burt Bacharach, as is well known, wrote many perennially favorite songs and movie themes. At the first rehearsal for his upcoming appearance at the Riviera Hotel, an interesting conversation developed with the Dick Palombi Orchestra.

Burt began rehearsing the band with a popular tune that he wrote having a brisk 7/4 time signature (seven quarter beats to a measure). As Palombi's precision band played the first phrase perfectly in 7/4 time, Burt's rhythm section added another beat! To correct the problem, the band played the phrase again with the same outcome. Burt and his musicians each time added another beat at the end!

Burt then exclaimed to the band, "Hey guys, you're not playing that right. It's 7/4 time. Here, let me show you."

As his rhythm section rolled their eyes, smiled and looked the other way, Burt counted,

"One two three four five six sev-EN. See, it's easy! One two three four five six sev-EN!" (this actually is EIGHT beats to the measure!).

*"Trumpet players are slaves
to the mouthpiece!"*

—Al Porcino, lead trumpet Stan Kenton Orchestra

*"This bone section (Flamingo Hotel
Orchestra) is like SNAP, CRACKLE and
POP. And I sure know which one I am!"*

—Bill Harris, jazz trombonist

Usually, every year at Christmas-time, an open house party for the Dick Palombi Riviera Hotel Orchestra was held at the leader's comfortable home. With hilarious results, as the night wore on there soon unfolded a story repeated countless times by band members.

As the musicians, with their dates sat in a beautifully decorated room nursing their drinks, the family cat, unconcerned with all the festivities, strolled by.

The family's elderly grandfather, after scatting the cat off the nearby sofa, also strolled by, following the furry pet into another room as he made an off-the-cuff, innocent comment, "That damned cat sucks on EVERYTHING!"

The room became instantly quiet as everyone's personal fantasy thoughts ran rampant through their mind.

Finally, after a few breathless moments, from a corner of the room came the quiet voice of the drummer, "Heeeerrrrre, kitty kitty kitty!"

♫

Question asked of a musician on a cruise ship in the middle of the ocean, "Do all you musicians live on the ship?"

♫

One of the Riviera Orchestra's bachelor musicians was known to patrol the hotel bar every night after the last show, "checking the traps," hoping to get lucky and find a little companionship for the night.

One night, after several unsuccessful hits, he

thought himself lucky as he talked to a friendly young tourist from the Midwest. With drinks flowing and lively conversation happening, things certainly looked very promising until she suddenly sat up very straight and exclaimed:

"Is your name ******* ******?

My mother warned me about you! I'm outta here!"

♫

Jazz trumpeter Dizzy Gillespie, while appearing at an International Trumpet Convention in Reno one year, was interviewed by a pseudo-hip young trumpet player, "Which trumpet players play the best, West or East Coast?" he asked.

Diz answered, "Well, West Coast trumpet players don't play nearly as well as East Coast trumpet players think they do!"

♫

As the popular Denver-based Dean Bushnell Orchestra performed at an annual party for the local Elks Club, the somber hour of 11:00 p.m. arrived when Elks traditionally honor their fallen members.

As the chimes tolled eleven dramatic strikes, the ceremony began with a full-sized, stuffed elk being wheeled onstage.

To the complete horror of Elk members and band-leader alike, they watched as a tipsy saxophonist came riding out astride the elk!

Failing to see the humor in that event, the club manager unceremoniously fired the band for the gig next year.

♪

A well known vibraphonist and percussionist in the Nat Brandwynne Caesars Palace Orchestra would often play, in a darkened orchestra pit, a particular vibes solo that accompanied scenes onstage.

Being supremely confident in the knowledge of his instrument and the setup of bars on his vibra-phone, he would make a quick move in the dark from the timpani to vibes, and begin his usually well played beautiful solo.

One night though, a turn of events occurred that left the band almost paralyzed with laughter. Someone, arriving onstage early had apparently rearranged all the vibes tone bars, switching this bar for that, low note bars for high ones, until the very unmusical instrument became just a collection of noisy metal.

At the very first note, the shocked vibist realized something was amiss, but it was too late to do anything but continue and the solo became quite bizarre!

With suspicious looks all around, the vibist glared at the band, but the culprit was unfortunately never found.

♫

Bessie Smith, a real old time shouting blues singer from the 1920s and '30s, recorded a song that had very funny, but racy lyrics for that day and age.

Called "My Kitchen Man," it became an instant hit around the country, but according to the 1929 copyright statement, it could be sung only at night, apparently after the kiddies had gone to bed.

The lyrics are as follows:

"I love his succotash

He's my kitchen man

He can use my sugar bowl anytime

He's my kitchen man

His frankfurters are so sweet

I love his sausage meat!"

♫

Bob Hope's comment on the then-president Harry Truman,

"He rules the country with an iron fist, the same way he plays piano!"

CHAPTER EIGHT

ONCE MORE FROM THE TOP

DURING A LARGE formal banquet, jazz pianist Lou Levy raised his wine glass and offered this toast:

> *"Here's to all the musicians who have died coming out of the bridge to "Sophisticated Lady."*

The long running Merv Griffin TV show of the 1970s, starring its durable talk show host Merv Griffin, was often filmed at the International Hotel (later the Hilton.) The usual cast centered around the fine band of leader Mort Lindsey with a personnel that included, among others, a very witty jazz trumpeter, Jack Sheldon.

On one memorable occasion, as the band rehearsed the program for the upcoming show, included in the lineup was Chita Rivera, a talented dancer whose flamenco-style music featured several difficult trumpet passages. Ably supported by fellow trumpeters Bill Hodges and Bill Berry, Jack appeared to be struggling somewhat with the tricky first trumpet part of the florid Spanish music.

When asked by the bandleader, "Jack, Is that part going to be okay on the show today?"

Without a moment's hesitation Jack answered,

"Are you kidding? If I could play that, would I be in THIS band?"

♫

Famed guitarist Chet Atkins, in an interview once said, "When I was a little boy, I told my dad that when I grew up I wanted to be a musician."

Dad answered, "Son, you can't do both!"

♫

On a long cross country tour of movie theatres after the end of WW II, irrepressible practical jokester jazz violinist Joe Venuti found himself doing a series of

Saturday morning movie matinees for the kiddies, teamed for some unexplainable reason with cowboy movie star Roy Rogers and Trigger, "The Smartest Horse in the Movies."

As do many performers, Joe had an incredible ego that matched his larger-than-life personality, and quickly found it hard to cope with the fact that on the theatre marquee, Trigger had top billing over himself. After weeks of stewing and fuming, Joe set in motion a plan to rectify the situation. Trigger, always the kids' favorite, was a virile stud horse with all his original plumbing intact and understandably could be quite excitable.

During one performance while Roy was onstage singing his heart out and finishing his last tune, he as usual turned and whistled to Trigger to make his entrance. In the wings offstage, unknown to Roy, the devilish Venuti had been tickling with his violin bow the genitalia of the easily excitable horse!

On hearing Roy's whistle, out thundered Trigger to the spotlight, prancing and snorting in all his erect "studly" glory. Amid the stifled gasps of Moms in the audience, there were many snickers and giggles from a thousand wide-eyed youngsters!

Offstage, Venuti chuckled to himself as he enjoyed his sweet revenge!

*"Too many pieces of music finish way
too long after the end!"*
—Igor Stravinsky, "Rite of Spring" composer

Musicians in Vegas, looking for other sorts of relaxation after performing demanding shows, formed a baseball team that was part of a citywide casino league. To escape the oppressive summertime heat, competitive games were often played at night when the majority of team members were off work. Along with musicians, various other teams were made up of dealers, waiters, stagehands and busboys.

At two o'clock in the morning, with ball field lights blazing and stands filled with screaming spouses, lively games would often last until the morning sun. Then to home and bed for most of the morning.

Luckily, ball scores were not as important as good exercise.

♫

To a struggling young cellist at rehearsal, Sir Thomas Beecham, the salty conductor extraordinaire of

London's Royal Philharmonic Orchestra, once remarked, "Young lady, between your legs you have the most beautiful instrument in the world, and all you can do is scratch it!"

♫

The gorgeous Stardust Hotel became a well known showcase for exciting production shows like the "Lido de Paris." Together with a big orchestra, a large company of dancers and singers with jugglers, acrobats and animal acts to enliven the stage, every night promised a new experience.

For example, one elaborate scene featured two large warhorses ridden bareback by Roman gladiators. For dozens of previous shows, everything had gone exactly as rehearsed. The two horsemen would ride their mounts to center stage from opposite sides, and turning sharply would head straight toward the audience at full gallop. At the last moment, the riders would rein in their sweating steeds, leaving them standing with flared nostrils over the front tables of the audience. It was most certainly a breathtaking scene.

One night though, things went badly amiss. To excite the horses for a dramatic show biz effect, it was later found that offstage the trainers had been tapping the horses on the rumps with small sticks embedded with tiny nails to make their nostrils flare!

Together with that, as the horses reached center stage to wheel and gallop toward the audience, one of the riders FELL OFF!

The big horse, expecting to be reined in as usual, galloped on at full speed right off the edge of the stage onto a large table seated with dozens of people.

(As comedian Shecky Greene later commented in his own show at the Riviera, "Waiter, I ordered roast beef!")

Incredibly, when paramedics were called, neither horse nor patron was injured, but it certainly made for a night to be remembered.

During the whole uproar, the band, of course, was told to keep playing and playing and playing.

♪

One trombone player to another, "See that trumpet player over there? He has perfect ears! Yeah, no holes in 'em!"

♪

Dr. Si Zentner, famous trombonist / bandleader at a recent concert with his band, heard a loud heckler yelling to the band, "What ever happened to Kay

Kyser, that old bandleader in the 1950s?"

Salty Si's quick response, "NOT NEARLY ENOUGH!"

♪

Famed guitarist Chet Atkins, sporting his brand new glasses, emerged from the men's restroom and remarked to his friends,

"I was standing at the urinal with my new bi-focals admiring the big one while the LITTLE one was peeing on my foot!"

♪

Singer Ray Charles, during a rehearsal for his new show at the Thunderbird Hotel, stopped the band saying, "We've gotta check a wrong note back there in the trumpets."

One of the trumpet players spoke up, "Ray, we've played this for days. There's no wrong note in that section."

Ray then answered, "Man, I'm telling you there is a wrong note. I'm BLIND. I ain't f***ing deaf!"

*"Wagner's music is much better
than it sounds!"*

—William Nye, newspaper columnist)

Often appearing in Vegas showrooms, singer Ray Charles showed his witty side as he boarded a airline flight dressed in an official pilot's uniform. Together with dark glasses and white cane as he tapped his way down the aisle to the cockpit, he remarked,

"Good morning folks. I'm going to be your pilot today!"

♫

High note trumpeter Bill Chase formed a five-trumpet plus rhythm jazz group called "CHASE" during his stint in Vegas. As demand for the popular group quickly grew, festivals and tours were soon booked in several out of the way places.

While on one of those festival tours in South Africa, there unfolded an event that was almost beyond belief!

Bill and several band members decided on a photographic safari trip to one of the national parks. Always a camera fan, Bill had the fine long lensed equipment necessary, but one of the other trumpeters brought along the very worst choice of cameras for such a trip. A large, noisy, simple, old fashioned Polaroid!

While the hardy group bounced along in a jeep with their tour guide, a rhinoceros was spotted not too far away in the brush. With his ample warnings to "Stay close," the guide allowed riders to get out of the jeep for photo shoots.

As the Polaroid-toting musician crept through the brush trying for a closeup shot, the nearsighted rhino, hearing strange noises, became a little uneasy. The loud SNAP of the Polaroid's shutter disturbed him even more, and with perked up ears, the annoyed rhino menacingly trotted toward the sound. At that moment the trumpeter pulled the film sheet out of the camera with its loud ZIPP-SLAP!

After seeing the 3,000-pound animal starting to move faster toward the strange sound, the near frantic guide screamed, "RUN, RUNNN, RUUNN-NNNN!"

With a very angry rhino hot on his heels, the trumpeter raced through the brush, all the while looking at his upraised wristwatch as he timed the 60 seconds needed for the Polaroid exposure!

For musicians, timing is everything!

♫

Traveling bands sometimes were required to play under difficult conditions beyond their control.

On the famous New Jersey Steele Pier that jutted far out into the ocean, spray would sometimes fly up through an open spot in the back of the bandstand, drenching the trumpet section.

The Tommy Dorsey band, conducted by Sam Donahue, performed In South Carolina for dances often held in tobacco warehouses. Structures like these were built with wide slits in the floor to allow smoke to rise up to dry hanging leaves of tobacco. Dancers and musicians had to step lightly, but it sometimes proved to be a hazardous place.

In the Midwest during one winter tour, the Woody Herman orchestra played in a large unheated building in the middle of an empty cotton field.

Five minutes before the dance began, no cars were in the parking area, but as the dance time approached, the parking area wondrously filled with a bustling scene.

In the near zero temperature, couples dancing around the red hot pot-bellied stove in the very center of the dance floor, found it better to keep moving rather than sitting and chatting with friends.

Wrapped up like Eskimos, the band, set up in the

far corner of the building, wore every heavy coat and fur cap they could find.

Five minutes after the dance ended, not one car remained in the parking lot!

♫

Before jazz trumpeter Red Rodney found a home in Las Vegas, he made forays into the be-bop world with the band of jazz saxophonist Charlie "Bird" Parker.

After the first phone call from Bird, this little redheaded Jewish kid from Philly happily journeyed to a city somewhere in the South to join the group.

As he joined the band for a concert in the heavily segregated town, he found that white musicians were not allowed to stay in the same hotels or to perform onstage with their African-American buddies.

Not knowing exactly what to do next, Red stealthily crouched down in the car seat and arrived at the concert hall in time to meet with the jazz saxophonist while they devised a solution.

Later in the concert, the trumpeter was introduced by Parker as "Albino Red, my cousin from Philadelphia, and he's going to sing a blues tune for you!"

Despite never being Albino Red before and never before singing a single tune, Red pulled it off just fine and enjoyed working with the band for quite a long time!

♫

As a young trumpet player was struggling with a complex solo, an unsympathetic conductor asked, "Why do you make that solo sound so hard?"

♫

Funny situations sometimes happen in unexpected places in the lives of working musicians. Take for example, these events that occurred in, of all places, a major prison near Chicago.

The Tommy Dorsey band, conducted by saxophonist Sam Donahue, was hired by the Illinois State Prison System to play a series of concerts at the Cook County State Prison.

As their bus arrived at the heavily guarded entrance, band members were escorted individually into lock-down areas, where they were searched carefully for weapons, contraband liquor, aspirin, medications, etc. With the primary search done, they were sent to another lock-down area to be completely searched a second time. Finally, members were sent to a third area for a more thorough search, and as nothing out of the ordinary was found, the band was able to make their preparations for the concerts.

Concert time quickly approached with the auditorium filling with inmates trooping in traditional lockstep. As band members looked around the large room, they noticed several high towers with guards bristling with machine guns. Their lighthearted attitude was dampened considerably.

Performing three long concerts over a period of twelve hours made for an exhausting day, and the band gladly found the chance to relax and dine with the guards. Despite the prisoners' idea that food in the guards' dining hall must be akin to dining in a gourmet restaurant, steaks there proved to be as tough as the guards' demeanor!

In a completely relaxed and friendly atmosphere, Dorsey band players found members of the prison band eager to talk music and to hear news of the outside music world.

The prison band was a fairly large-sized one, containing quite a few players who had been sentenced to jail terms of varying lengths. Musical Inmates soon found, that as long as they rehearsed, they could remain out of their cells, and quite naturally, they practiced like crazy all day long.

An interesting sidebar of the Dorsey band's visit, was that there was a prison newspaper published by inmates. Including a newsy column that featured a "Prisoner of the week" interview along with a photo, the paper was a bright spot in a normal gray prison day, as it offered the profile of a selected inmate.

With tongue in cheek humor, details like the following were prominently displayed in every edition, "Meet our Prisoner of the Week, Joe Smith.

Recently transferred from San Quentin, Joe is serving 20 years to life for assault, armed robbery and triple murder.

Joe's favorite hobby: Cross country running!"

♫

During the 1950s, jazz violinist Joe Venuti was the featured soloist on a network live TV show sponsored by a famous brand of men's hair cream.

As Joe finished a brilliant chorus on a popular tune of the day, he looked straight into the camera lens, lowered his head and pointed to his bald spot exclaiming, "Folks, just look at what this sponsor's product did to MY head!"

The TV screen quickly went dark as the sponsor pulled the plug!

CHAPTER NINE

THE GOOD 'OL BAD 'OL DAYS

*"It's taken all my life to learn
what not to play!"*
—Dizzy Gillespie, Jazz trumpeter

ALONG WITH MANY other hotel / casinos in Vegas, the beautiful Stardust Hotel soon became known as a fine showcase for the Donn Arden dancers in grand production shows such as the long running "Lido de Paris." Sometimes though, unexpected events like the following do occur.

During the quietest part of the show, with stage

lights softened for a delicate love scene between two lovers at center stage, the piano player, to set the mood rendered a quiet solo melody in the background. The large Eddie O'Neal Orchestra, with no music for that scene, sat quietly in the shadows of their offstage pit area, while the bandleader allowed his mind to drift away, thinking perhaps of being on a nice sunny vacation in Bermuda.

Suddenly the conductor, groggily coming out of his fog, leaped to his feet, and wrongly believing that they were in a different spot in the music, gave a gigantic downbeat in the quietest part of the scene. (Large downbeats always are followed by loud notes from an orchestra!)

With the quick movement of the downbeat continuing relentlessly downward, the leader soon woke up to the fact that he was not in the same musical spot with either the show or the band. When at last his downstroke reached the bottom, he quickly held out both palms and loudly yelled, "DON'T PLAY!"

As musicians tried to suck back in air, many mouthpieces were nearly swallowed that night!

♫

Joe Venuti's fame as one of the first be-bopper jazz violinists will live on for many years, as will his off-the-wall sense of humor. With some of his antics being a little too racy to be printable, there remains at least one more to be included.

Always the consummate jazz artist with impeccable time, Joe had an immediate dislike for anyone who patted his foot loudly while playing.

On one gig, when teamed with a very heavy-footed and equally out of time bass player, Joe could stand it no longer. During one of his co-performer's interminable jazz choruses, Joe strolled offstage, secured hammer and nails from a stagehand, then gleefully nailed the surprised offender's wingtip shoe to the stage!

He then growled, "Now, let's see you pat your f***-ing foot with that!"

♫

Comedians thrive on good audience response, and as a result sometimes fall into the routine of doing the exact same tried and true jokes that get the biggest laughs every night.

Take for example that huge star, Milton Berle, whose career spanned many years working in vaudeville, having had his own long running TV show called the Texaco Star Hour, and later appearing multiple times in Vegas.

Labeled "The Thief of Badgags," Berle claimed to have over one million gags in his expansive library, yet he always relied on a few select time-worn jokes and routines. The showbands working many times with him came to know the routines almost as well as "Uncle Miltie."

After taking a vacation of several weeks, Milton returned to a rehearsal with the Dick Palombi Riviera Orchestra, and failing to remember his next move in an old routine, he quizzed his conductor as to what to do next.

Almost in a single voice, the entire band quickly said, "You walk to the other side of the stage and then turn right, Milton!"

Berle responded, "You're right, guys. I forgot my own act!"

"It was said that Guy Lombardo
died with his mutes on!"
—Glenn Shull, lead trombonist

Tenor man Bob Seidell's vivid descriptions of the musicians around him have given local players much to chuckle about over the years. Bob's stiletto sharp wit skewered to the band room walls many an unsuspecting not-so-professional player, leaving no one safe and nothing too sacred to escape his pointed jabs.

For instance, Bob might outline his all-star dream band, while working in Lake Tahoe with bandleader "Dempsey Dipstick" and his "Ptomaine Tempos" at "Harry's under-the-Pines."

The orchestra, sometimes conducted by "Dudley Do-Right," "Snidely Whiplash" or "Radar Rod" might accompany a "Tits and Feathers Show" produced by "Frederick Flatcar," starring a line of dancers called "the Horizontal Ballet," and a duo of operatic singers called "Bellows Lugosi" and "Cynthia Screech."

The stellar trumpet section might include "Sylvester Switchpitch, "Kosher Dillon" and "Jose' Heat," while the bone section could be made up of "Waldo Weirdbeard," "Woody Hermit," and "Silent Yokum."

Rounding out the horn section were reed players "John Crueltone," "the Coleman Hawkins of the Wilhelm-Strasse," "Sydney Stroboscope," and "Freddie and his Cobraphone," while the rhythm section might include "the Orangutan of the Piano," a drummer labeled as "the Boiler Maker," bassist "Felonious Thump," and percussionist "The Village Whitesmith."

Occasionally added to the band were an accordionist named "Art van Dumb" or the "Synagogue Soprano and his "Cacophonous Calliope." As usual, following every successful gig, there might be a band party, if okayed by the band accountants "The Clutchpenny Brothers" and their "Accounts Deceivable," and if the bandleader "Uncle Wiggley and his Child Bride" would spring for it.

"You have to save up for these gigs!"
—Lester Young, Jazz saxophonist

Not to be outdone with productions of large shows, the New Frontier Hotel presented its own mini-production that included elaborate staging and a fairly large company of singers and dancers.

Because of limited space onstage, the Dick Rice house band, rather than being in an orchestra pit, was placed in an area at the side of the stage in the audience. The elevator type pit allowed dancers quick up and down access to dressing rooms for costume changes during the show. A stagehand in charge of the elevator would push the "down" button, sending it to a lower level with the dancers and then immediately would return it to its "up" position.

One night though, things rapidly went amiss as the busy stagehand failed to return the elevator to its normal "up" position.

Onstage, as the featured lady performer sang the last high note in her rousing rendition of "The Italian Street Song," with her face bathed in a blinding pin spot on a completely dark stage, she took a step forward into nothingness!

Luckily the pit elevator remained only a few feet down at the time, but still this was a substantial jolt in the dark. Although the lady was later found to be bruised but unhurt, loud moans and groans were soon heard coming from the pit.

As lights came on and the worried audience stood to see into the pit, someone yelled: "Oh my god! Somebody do something quick! Play the Star Spangled Banner!"

♫

Heard from a sideman during a band rehearsal:

*"Boss, you're not going to play this
music around open food, are you?"*
—Bob Seidell, saxophonist

In the '70's and '80's, major hotels were more than glad to provide the large backup orchestras that big stars commanded. Singers like Tony Bennett performed with an expanded 95-piece Joe Guercio string section at the Hilton, Andy Williams with the 48-piece Nat Brandwynne Caesars Palace Orchestra and Frank Sinatra, not to be outshone, did his thing with the large impressive orchestra of Antonio Morelli at the Sands Hotel.

Around this period of time though, a few seemingly irreconcilable problems surfaced between Sinatra and the Sands.

Becoming more than just a little miffed because of a gaming misunderstanding, Sinatra cancelled his contract and then drove a golfcart straight through the very large expensive plate glass window at the front of the hotel!

♫

The irrepressible comedian Jack Benny, with his outstanding sense of humor, appeared many times over the years in the luxurious Caesars Palace showroom.

During many performances in his opening monologue, Jack spoke lovingly about appearing with major symphonies and other orchestras around the country, playing his violin to raise money for charity.

Finally promising, although some would say threatening, to display his talent and play for the audience, Jack turned to the wings of the stage and asked a stagehand,

" Would you please bring out my STRADIVARIUS violin to me?"

The stagehand, who without doubt, must have been a retired pro-basketball player, because at every performance, he unerringly tossed the violin 35 feet to land at Benny's feet!

After looking at the scattered pieces of violin at his feet, Benny did one of his very long trademark pauses, and then said,

"If that's my Strad, I guess I'm out the fifty dollars I paid Mitsubishi."

♫

The Tommy Dorsey band, after Tommy's death, was conducted by saxophonist Sam Donahue, and while on one of its extensive travels throughout the south, the band bus arrived one day at the air base at Cape Canaveral for their gig at the officers' club.

At the base entry gate, the armed guard gave precise directions to the officers' club,

"Travel straight ahead for two miles where you will come to a wide boulevard. Make a left turn and travel one mile and you will find a large building in front of you. That's the officers' club."

The confident bus driver, following the careful directions, drove to the first wide boulevard, made a hard left and proceeded on for about a half mile. Finally, the bandleader, seeing a very tall building directly ahead, told the driver,

"That's it. It sure is a huge building, but that's got to be the officers' club."

Suddenly, sirens screamed and blinking red lights flashed as an armored personnel carrier, bristling with fifty-caliber machine guns aimed at the bus, barred the way. Armed air police in heavy gear with menacing dogs quickly surrounded the bus and stormed on board.

After some intense conversation and producing of identification, the leader convinced the air police that this was not a terrorist attack, but simply a band bus on the way to the gig.

The bus, apparently in making a hard left turn,

had driven down the wrong wide boulevard which led to the heavily guarded huge building, where were kept, tall Redstone rockets intended for moon shots!

"I went on the road with the Stan Kenton Orchestra to get a reputation, and I got one. As a drunk!"

—John Carroll, lead trumpet Stan Kenton Orchestra

Opening nights for shows can sometimes become near disasters and alert audiences often would attend just to see those miscues. Dancers, perhaps in wrong positions, costume slipups, scenery malfunctions, and band problems, sometimes happened on opening nights.

Take for example this event at Caesars Palace on the opening night of one elaborate show.

One show producer's novel idea placed the large onstage orchestra on a movable platform on wheels. Propelled by an electric motor, this cart was controlled electronically by a stagehand who slowly moved it to different positions around the stage. At least that was the original plan!

During the opening night show, things quickly went awry as hand controls for the electric band cart failed to respond. As the cart, loaded with the large 35-piece orchestra sitting at their places on raised tiers, slowly moved from the back of the stage toward the audience, the stagehand with the hand-held control frantically pushed the "stop" button. But nothing happened!

As the heavy cart moved forward relentlessly toward the front edge of the stage, the audience, with good reason, became more concerned with every passing moment. This certainly was not the sort of excitement hoped for on opening night.

Seemingly with nothing able to stop the relentless onward movement of the cart, the band realized that now might be a prudent time to abandon ship, and started gathering up their prized instruments.

As showgoers down front began seriously looking for safer places, the momentum of the cart was stopped just in time when its front wheels luckily dropped off the edge of the stage.

Many big sighs of relief were heard from audience and band alike, as stagehands retrieved the errant cart and at last the show continued.

♫

That outstanding trombonist, Tommy Dorsey never found time to put together his own trombone before performing. One of the other musicians was paid to do that for him. Tommy would then come on stage, and without warming up, play his demanding theme song, "Getting Sentimental Over You."

One night, as the sideman was assembling the horn for Tommy, he accidentally bumped the trombone slide, causing a small dent which prevented the smooth movement of the slide.

Fearfully hoping that the leader would not notice the problem, he carefully placed the horn on its stand and took his place in the band.

As Tommy walked on stage, he picked up his horn, gave a quick movement of the slide and said loudly, "OHHH YEAH!"

Glaring daggers at the offending sideman, Tommy then chased him into the parking lot, cursing and threatening to tear him limb from limb!

CHAPTER TEN

VIVA LAS VEGAS

"Jazz is the thinking man's music."
—Duke Ellington, bandleader

WHEN SAXOPHONIST Bob Seidell, with his rapier sharp wit first swooped into "Tinsel Town" along with his "Sobbing Selmer," the vocabulary of working musicians took a quantum leap. No one was safe from his caustic wit and pointed jabs. For example, one accordion player / leader he worked for became "Bellows Lugosi" or "Art Van Clam and his Belly Baldwin!" "Sammy Suctionshoes" or "Melvin

Manglemeter" were nicknames less affectionately given to a well known singer whose shows always ran overtime while he almost destroyed the rhythm of a song by jumping measures and losing meter. Lead trumpeters who usually played the melody along with the singer to help him stay on pitch were instructed to point the trumpet at the back of the singer's head following him wherever he moved around the stage while singing.

There were trumpeters who fit the names of "Vernon Vaguevalve," "Disney Gillespie" and "Sylvester Switchpitch?" Leaders became known known as "Old Mothwallets" or a drummer called "Simon Slamcymbal?" Bass players became "Felonius Thump" and girl singers invariably were "Cynthia Screech," along with piano players who were the "Blacksmiths of the piano."

Being an equal opportunity slasher, while working in Reno, Bob glibly labeled one orchestra leader the "Lester Lanin of the Luftwaffe." One violinist became "Jascha Halfwitz," another "The Thief of Badstrad," a duo of cellists "Pablo Cackles" and "Annette Funnycello" and a line of dancers "The Stretchmark Sisters!"

No one was safe from Seidell's pointed jabs.

♫

Before the above mentioned saxophone player went to "that Great Bandroom in the Sky," he had the opportunity in Las Vegas to work with a band-leader who, although being very short in stature, had a king-sized ego, "Little Sir Ego." This "Man Who came to Hinder" conducted one of the large production shows in "Titsneyland" at the Tropicana, and was rather infamous for always wearing a "rug" that looked something akin to a road killed possum.

Out of the complete boredom of doing the exact same show every night hundreds of times, the dancers took fiendish delight in trying to dislodge the leader's rug as they twirled and whirled every night around the passarelle in their weighted ballroom gowns. The orchestra pit, as usual, was lower than the stage, and by necessity the conductor's head was exposed somewhat as he followed the events unfolding onstage.

One night, the inevitable did happen as a lucky flip of a showgirl's skirt caught the leader's rug, pushing it down over his eyes leaving the band snickering, the dancers guffawing and the leader muttering and fuming!

♫

With so many shows being produced, work was plentiful and as the work load increased, talented musicians craved other outlets for creative expression. To relieve the boredom of playing the same shows night after night, they looked for places to play music that they chose.

Rehearsal bands, or kicks bands as they were known, sprang into being with night spots like the Black Magic, the Torch Club, the Carver House, the Colonial House, and Club La Vista all becoming places available for a little artistic expression.

Often with informal concerts starting around 2 a.m. and lasting until the sun came up, crowds of off work dancers, singers and musicians flocked there for a few brews and much needed relaxation.

♫

Conrad Gozzo, a highly respected first trumpeter in the recording studios of Los Angeles for many years, was well known for playing his trademark "big fat notes" even when the original notation was marked "short."

Once during a recording session with Billy May's band, the leader stopped the session and exclaimed,

"Hey Goz, can you play that last note shooooooooooort!"

♪

The "Fabulous" Flamingo Hotel was noted for bringing in swingin' big bands into their fan-friendly lounge, and the large crowds of jazz lovers showed their appreciation. Big bands, such as those of Count Basie, Duke Ellington, Harry James, Tommy Dorsey conducted by Sam Donahue, Buddy Rich, and Woody Herman manned the stage and drew eager crowds, who like sponges soaked up good beer and good music.

♪

The much publicized opening in the mid-fifties of the stylishly modern Moulin Rouge Hotel promised a new era for hotels in Vegas. Other hotel owners on the Strip watched carefully as large mixed crowds attended the opening performances of "Tropi-CanCan." Along with its small, but mighty pit orchestra, the show became an instant success with attendance healthy.

Being the first completely integrated hotel/casino in the United States, the friendly atmosphere welcomed singers and musicians of all persuasion, and soon became a favorite spot for after hour jam sessions. It became 'THE" place to go and be seen.

Because of its lasting impact, the hotel, although

destroyed by fire a few years later, was listed on "The United States National Register of Historic Places."

♫

After working hard every night on their gigs, there were a few bandleaders who in their off hours, came to be noted as more than merely social drinkers.

Two such big drinking buddies were long time residents of Las Vegas, bandleader/trumpeter Harry James and Louis Prima, another bandleader/trumpeter. Their homes situated on the beautiful Desert Inn golf course sat comfortably next to each other.

Oftentimes, after their respective gigs for the night were finished, the two buds, along with Betty Grable, Harry's pinup girl movie star wife and Keeley Smith, Prima's talented singer wife, would meet at a local all-night supermarket for some late night shopping, a not uncommon summertime activity for musicians in Las Vegas.

Apparently though, several generous helpings of the bubbly proved to always bring out the inner boy in both men and their antics sometimes got them in trouble. Take for example, this:

As the two couples were doing their shopping and walking down the aisles, they came to the canned vegetable department and spied a very tall pyramid of neatly stacked canned veggies on the floor. The temptation was just too much for Louis.

"Hey Harry, watch this!" Prima yelled, as he went flying through the air in a big spread eagle leap into the middle of the stack. Cans scattered here and there like so many dropped marbles, while irritated grocery clerks looked on in disgust.

Not to be outdone, Harry then yelled to Prima "Oh yeah, Louis, just watch this" as he leaped in the air, landing right in the middle of a large beautifully displayed arrangement of bananas, apples and oranges. Immediately it became squashed fruit salad!

Enough was enough for the irate store manager, as he quickly escorted the gleeful duo with their mortified wives from the store!

As a result, Harry and Louis were "eighty-sixed" from the grocery store (a Vegas term meaning "Don't ever darken our door again!").

♫

Johnny Long band singer Debbie Brown, to a lady gushing about how marvelous it must be to travel on a band bus with all those men, "It's just fifteen different smells!"

♫

"Hockeypuck" was an affectionate nickname given to a percussionist hired by the Russ Black Orchestra as an added man to do the Danny Thomas show at the Flamingo Hotel.

Each night at showtime, as was his usual routine, Thomas would take a tumbler of fine scotch on stage with him to sip as he did his opening monologue part of the show. One memorable night though, he forgot his drink, and starting to feel a little hoarse, signaled to his valet offstage to send out a glass of his favorite Chivis Regal "throat saver."

Quickly served up by the valet, the scotch tumbler passed through the band without spilling a drop, until it came to Hockeypuck, the last man in line. In paying no attention to what had been said on stage, Hockeypuck must have thought that this booze was a gift from heaven, as he quickly disposed of it down his open gullet!

By this time, a fidgeting Thomas wondered where his drink was and the valet waving his arms in bewilderment sent out another, Passing again from hand to hand through the band, it finally reached the end of the line again. Hockeypuck, who no doubt thought "How lucky am I?" quickly drank that one also.

By now, Thomas was really agitated saying to the

puzzled valet: "What's going on? Send me out the scotch!" Out came the scotch for the third time, hand to hand to Hockeypuck, who by then was starting to feel no pain. He downed the third glass even quicker than before, and then fell with a big thump off his drum stool.

With all attempts failing to get him quietly off the bandstand, security guards finally reached under the rear curtain and dragged him off by the ankles giggling, smiling, and quite pleased with himself!

♫

Louis Prima, a longtime entertainer in the Desert Inn lounge with his wife, singer Keeley Smith and bandleader Sam Butera and the Witnesses, gained lasting fame as the composer of Benny Goodman's pre-wartime hit "Sing, Sing, Sing." It's a tune still popular with the younger dance crowd after over 80 years.

♫

The 1992 movie, "Honeymoon in Las Vegas" starring James Caan, Nicholas Cage, and Sarah Jessica Parker, was filmed in Vegas with a supporting cast that included the ten-man "Flying Elvi" skydive team and ONE THOUSAND Elvis impersonators!

Elvis wannabes of every race, color, size, shape, and gender, both air borne and earth bound, were invited to appear in the movie and it was truly amazing to see that over 1,000 responded. With no boundaries set, there were Elvises tall, short, male, female, adult, children, Asian, African-American, Caucasian and Latino, who happily donned their flashy sparkly white costumes and strutted their stuff for the cameras.

After the day's filming was in the can, many hundreds of those same impersonators staked out their spots on the Vegas Strip, and with boom boxes blasting out "You Ain't Nothing But A Hound Dog," they curled their upper lips, straightened their black wigs, and did their best imitation of the "King."

The admiring crowds were swamped with every imaginable version of the man from Memphis.

♫

Clark Terry, one of the most innovative and distinctive trumpet players of our time, used an assortment of mutes in his jazz choruses. Jazzers often used such unusual things as felt hats, water glasses, coconut shells, bucket mutes, and plungers to give a different sound to their choruses.

Clark's favorite was the soft rubber end of a

toilet plunger. When used, the trumpet would then produce the "wa-wa" sound that blues players through the years used so effectively.

On one of his many solo tours, Terry somehow misplaced his prized plunger mute, so he quickly made the necessary trip to a local hardware store for a replacement. Being met at the front door by a helpful young clerk, Terry was guided to the plumbing department where he began sorting through a box of useful supplies.

After finding the perfect rubber part, Terry began making his way to the cashier when the young clerk exclaimed, "Don't you want the stick that goes with it?"

"I never use one!" answered the trumpeter.

"Geeze," said the incredulous clerk, "That's disgusting!"

♫

Latino wedding receptions are mostly friendly affairs, where both families join together to hire a suitable orchestra, engage a caterer, rent a ballroom for the afternoon, and invite the entire neighborhood.

On one such happy occasion in Phoenix, as the Pete Bugarin Latin Band played its first tunes, the caterers busily prepared the food buffet tables directly in front of the stage. Cold cans of cerveza could be heard popping open around the old Riverside ballroom as hungry friends lined up in rows to sample the food.

Unexpectedly though, events quickly took a turn for the worse.

As the fathers of both bride and groom reached the buffet table, one was heard to loudly growl, "My kid's too good for your kid!"

Then the big fight was on. When the fathers started punching each other, flinging insults, food, and beer bottles, most of the 500 guests also joined in the fray! Every guest there seemed to have a vocal/physical opinion about the whole affair.

The police riot squad responded quickly, and more than 50 party-goers celebrated the rest of the night in the city jail!

Taking its cue, the band hastily packed up and mambo-ed out the back stage door!

"I've been fired off better bands than this!"
—Jack Sheldon, jazz trumpeter

BIBLIOGRAPHY AND OTHER TITLES OF INTEREST

The Big Bands, George T. Simon, MacMillan Publishers

The Big Band Almanac, Leo Walker, Da Capo Press 1989

The Big Bands, Leo Walker, Da Capo Press

The Wonderful Era of the Great Dance Bands, Leo Walker, Howell North Books 1964

Music is My Mistress, Duke Ellington Autobiography, Da Capo Press 1973

Good Morning Blues, Count Basie Autobiography with Albert Murray, Da Capo Press

Leader of the Band, Woody Herman, Gene Lees , Oxford University Press

Woodchopper's Ball, Woody Herman autobiography, Limelight Pub.

Chronicle of the Herds, Bill Clancy, Schirmer Pub.

Buddy DeFranco, a Biographical Portrait, John Kuehn and Arne Alstrup, Scarecrow Press.Rutgers

Ah-one, Ah-two, Life with my Musical Family, Lawrence Welk, Prentice-Hall Books

Born to Swing, the Story of the Big Bands, Ean Wood, Sanctuary Pub l. LTD. Kent, England

Clifford Brown, The Life & Art of the Legendary Jazz Trumpeter, Rick Catalano, Oxford Univ. Press

The Jazz Scene, Francis Newton, MacGibbon and K, London

The Book of Jazz, Leonard Feather, Paper Back Library Horizon Press

MF Horn, Maynard Ferguson's Life in Music, Dr. Wm. F. Lee, MF Music USA

Understanding Jazz, Leroy Ostransky, Prentice Hall Books

Tommy and Jimmy, the Dorsey Years, Herb Sanford, Arlington House Press

Jazz, America's Classical Music, Grover Sales, Prentice-Hall Books

Ishkabibble, Merwyn Bogue Autobiography, Louisiana Univ. State Press

Odyssey of the Mid-Nite Flyer, Lee Barron, El Roy V. Lee Publishers

A Thousand Golden Horns, Gene Fernett, Pendell Co. Publishers

Miles, Autobiography, with Quincy Troupe , Simon and Schuster

Jazz Is, Nat Hentoff, Limelight Editions NYC

West Coast Jazz, Ted Gioia, Oxford Univ. Press

Jazz History, John Fordham, Dorland Kindersley Press London

Origin and Development of Jazz, Dr. Otto Werner Kendell Hunt Publishers 1984

Have Tux, Will Travel, Bob Hope, Simon and Schuster

Don't Shoot, It's Only Me, Bob Hope

Las Vegas is My Beat, Ralph Pearl

My Favorite Comedies in Music, Victor Borge

My Favorite Intermissions, Victor Borge

Jazz , Tanner Megill Gerow, Wm. C. Brown Publishers, London

Pictorial History of Jazz, Orrin Keepnews and Bill Grau, Bonanza Books NYC 1981

Las Vegas, as it Began, as it Grew, Stanley W. Paher, Nevada Publications 1971

When the Mob Ran Vegas, Steve Fischer Berkline Press

Tonight at Noon, Sue Graham Mingus, Pantheon Books

Magnificent Mendez, Dr. Jane Hickman, Summit Press Tempe

Sound of the Trumpet, Bill Moody, Waker & Co. 435 Hudson St. NYC

Solo Hand, Bill Moody, Walker & Co. 435 Hudson St. NYC

Death of a Tenor Man, Bill Moody, Walker $ Co. 435 Hudson St. NYC

Bird Lives, Bill Moody, Waker & Co. 435 Hudson St. NYC

Looking for Chet Baker, Bill Moody, Walker & Co. 435 Hudson St. NYC

Fade to Blue, Bill Moody, Walker & Co. 435 Hudson St. NYC

Shades of Blue, Bill Moody, Walker & Co. 435 Hudson St. NYC

Who's Who in Jazz, John Chilton

Born to Swing, Ean Wood

Jazz Scene, Francis Newton

Leon Merian, the Man Behind the Horn, Bill Bridges, Diem Publishers

Chet Baker, the Lost Memoirs....As Though I Had Wings, St. Martin's Griffin Press NYC

Lullabye of Birdland, George Shearing w/Alyn Shipton

A Century of Jazz, Roy Carr, Octopus Pub. Group, London, 1997

Jazz, John Fordham Dorland Kindersley, London, 1993

The Dance Band Era, Albert McCarthy November Books Ltn 1971

The Jazz Scene, Charles Fox Hamlyn Pub. Group, 1972

Played Out on the Strip, Janis L. McKay, Univ. of Nevada Press, Reno 2016

How I Became a Cornetist, Herbert L. Clarke..Brass Musician.com

Sam Noto, A Life in Jazz, Joey Giambra Self Publ.

The World of Jazz, Rodney Dale, Chartwell Books Inc. Edison New Jersey, 1996

Kenny Baker, the Life and times of a Jazz Musician, Robert Cosby Evergreen Pub.

The Origin and Development of Jazz, Otto Werner Kendall Hunt Pub. 1984

The Eye of Jazz, Herman Leonard, Viking Pen

ENTERTAINERS APPEARING IN VEGAS OVER THE YEARS

BECOMING KNOWN worldwide for having top quality precision orchestras, Las Vegas showrooms produced outstanding shows with a wide array of entertainers. The following is an incomplete list of those remarkable characters who found a home on the stages of Tinsel Town:

SINGERS

Elvis Presley
Sergio Franchi
Bobby Vinton
Tony Bennett
Rod Stewart
Perry Como
Frank Sinatra
Pearl Bailey
Helen Reddy
Frank Sinatra, Jr.
Harry Connick, Jr.
Nancy Sinatra
Tina Sinatra
Ennio Stuarti
Gianni Russo
Marvin Gaye
Roger Miller
Kris Kristofferson
Lee Greenwood
Matt Monroe
Mary Kaye Trio
John Davidson
Theodore Bikel
Guy Mitchell
Vaughn Monroe
The Coasters
The Mills Brothers
Sandler & Young
Frank DeRone
The Four Lads

Suzanne Summers
Smokey Robinson
The Four Aces
Susan Anton
Marilyn McCoo
Billy Davis
The Four Tops
The Fifth Dimension
Petula Clark
Ernie Andrews
James Brown
Sammy Davis, Jr.
Toni Tenille
Connie Francis
Vicki Carr
Ethel Merman
Tex Ritter
Bobby Gentry
Harry Belafonte
Joanie James
Dick Haymes, Jr.
Steve & Eydie
Gorme'
Charo
Paul Anka
Patti Page
Abbe Lane
Connie Stevens
Dolly Parton
Al Hibbler
Helen Forrest

Kenny Rogers
Bill Medley
Helen O'Connell
Eddie Arnold
Susan Hayward
Etta James
Kenny Rogers & 1st
Edition
Hildegarde
Dottie West
Polly Bergen
Rosemary Clooney
Frankie Avalon
Julius LaRosa
Ella Fitzgerald
Carol Lawrence
Bobby Rydell
Joanie O'Brien
Robert Goulet
Frankie Valli & 4
Seasons
The Lettermen
Pat Boone
Don Ho
Jimmy Rogers
Dick Jensen
Nat King Cole
Barry Manilow
Al Martino
Vic Damone
Frankie Laine

John Denver
Gordon McRae
Roberta Sherwood
Neil Diamond
Barbra McNair
Sheila McRae
Roberta Peters
Diahann Carroll
Fran Warren
Marty Robbins
The Kids Next Door
The Temptations
Jose' Feliciano
Ronnie Milsap
Johnny Mathis
Debbie Reynolds
Dorothy L'amour
June Christy
Ann Richards
Gatlin Brothers
Peaches & Herb
The Carpenters
Luther Vandross
Peggy Lee
Karen Carpenter
Richard Carpenter
Eddie Fisher
Judy Garland
Liza Minelli
Olivia Newton John
Julie London

Bobby Troup
Anne Murray
Pia Zadora
Englebert
Humperdinck
Carmen McRae
Bob Anderson
Andy Williams
Danny Thomas
Johnny Ray
Ray Charles
Bill Withers
Ray Eberle
Dave Rowland &
Sugar
The Modernaires
Bob Eberle
Sarah Vaughn
Jim Stafford
The Pied Pipers
Anita O'Day
Manhattan Transfer
Jerry Vale
Minnie Ripperton
Glenn Campbell
Tony Roma
Kay Stevens
Tennessee
Ernie Ford
The Treniers
The Village People

Eartha Kitt
Billy Eckstein
Joey Adams
Don Cornell
Don Cherry
Barbara Eden
The Hi Lo's
Jack Jones
The Ames Brothers
Barbra Streisand
Gladys Knight & the
Pips
Chubby Checker
Nelson Eddy
The Four Freshmen
The Righteous
Brothers
Gail Sherwood
Mel Tormé
Bill Medley
Joey Heatherton
The Amazing
Inkspots
The Fantastic
Inkspots
The Original Inkspots
The Spectacular
Inkspots
Tina Turner
Wayne Newton
Sergio Mendes

Brazil '66

Johnny Mann Singers

Ray Stevens

The Chansonnes de

Paris

Joel Grey

Paul Winters

Joe Williams

The Mammas &

Papas

Joanie Sommers

The Platters

The Maguire Sisters

Andy Gibb

The Four Tops

The Andrew Sisters

Phyllis Maguire

Roy Clark

Buddy Greco

Neil Sedaka

The Castro Brothers

The Castro Sisters

The Checkmates

Tony Orlando &

Dawn

Bernadette Peters

Paul Anka

Royal Phillipine

Singers

Rouvann

Anita Bryant

Tiny Tim

Line Renaud

Tito Guizar

Tony Martin

Eddie Cantor

Herb Jeffries

Kay Starr

Matt Dennis

Alice Faye

Dionne Warwick

Celine Dion

Elton John

Michael Bublé

Sonny and Cher

Cher

Liberace

Danny Gans

Keeley Smith

Louis Prima

Marlene Dietrich

Lena Horne

Dorothy Dandridge

Lola Falana

Tom Jones

Diana Ross

Willie Nelson

Bette Midler

Sting

Celeste Holmes

Arthur Prysock

The Williams

Brothers

The Captain and

Tenille

Cyndi Lauper

Al Green

Sheena Easton

Clint Holmes

Martina McBride

Bruce Springsteen

Gordon Lightfoot

Pavorotti

Patti LaBelle

Alicia Keyes

John Mellencamp

Randy Travis

Bob Dylan

Lee Ann Womack

Lyle Lovett

Ozzy Osbourne

Bonnie Raitt

Michael Bolton

Lionel Richie

Cleo Laine

Tony Danza

Peter, Paul & Mary

Rolling Stones

Kenny Loggins

The Beatles

Paul McCartney

Natalie Cole

Nat King Cole

Bobby Darren
Isaac Hayes
Barry White
Garth Brooks
Prince
Lou Rawls
Marty Robbins
Mel Tillis
Jim Neighbors

COMEDIANS

George Burns
Totie Fields
Milton Berle
Pat Buttram
Norm Crosby
Jimmy Dean
Jack Durant
Alan King
Dom DeLuise
Johnny Carson
Bill Cosby
Jimmy Walker
Jackie Mason
Shecky Greene
Richard Pryor
Pete Barbutti
The Ritz Brothers
Jack Benny
Nancy Austin
Woody Allen
Rochester

Rusty Warren
Bob Newhart
Steve Martin
Steve Allen
Bob Hope
The Smothers Bros.
Frankie Fontaine
Charlie Callas
Sophie Tucker
Buddy Hackett
Allen & Rossi
Hank Henry
Sandy Hackett
Sammy Shore
Jerry Colonna
Jack Carter
Cork Proctor
Jimmy Durante
Irv Benson
Joey Bishop
Foster Brooks
Rip Taylor
George Gobel
Nipsey Russell
Rowan & Martin
John Byner
Judy Tenuta
Red Skelton
Bill Dana
David Brenner
Pat Cooper

Red Buttons
Johnny Yew
Redd Foxx
Dick Shawn
Professor Backwards
Dean Martin
Yakov Smirnoff
Pigmeat Markum
Don Rickles
Bob & Ray
Tom Poston
Jerry Lewis
Tom Dreesen
Victor Borge
Jack Soo
Guy Masters
Joe E. Lewis
Jan Murray
George Kirby
Minnie Pearl
Harry Anderson
Artie Johnson
Joan Rivers
Dick Capri
Morrie Amsterdam
Dick VanDyke
Jerry VanDyke
Danny Kaye
Phil Harris
Henny Youngman
Shelley Berman

Andy Griffin
Penn & Teller
David Letterman
Flip Wilson
Rita Rudner
Pat Morita
Jerry Seinfeld
Robin Williams
Ray Romano
Jay Leno
Sinbad
Tim Conway
Harvey Korman
Dennis Miller
Kevin James
Howie Mandel
Gabe Kaplan
Louie Anderson
Noell Coward
Belle Barth
Phyllis Diller
Billy Crystal
Roseanne Barr
George Carlin
Eddie Murphy
Myron Cohen
Rodney Dangerfield
Bob Newhart

DANCERS

Chita Rivera
Gene Barry
George Maharias
Shirley MacLaine
Gwen Verdon
Deanna Durbin
The Step Brothers
The Nicholas Brothers
Juliet Prowse
Ann Margret
Rita Moreno
The Dunhills
Jacqueline Douget
BoJangles Robinson
June Taylor Dancers
Cyd Charisse
José Greco
Donn Arden Dancers
Eartha Kitt
Folklorico de Mexico

MAGICIANS, IMPRESSIONISTS, ACTORS AND ACROBATS

Harry Blackstone
Blackstone, Jr.
Senor Wences
David Copperfield
Sigfried & Roy

Frank Gorshin
Rich Little
Wolfman Jack
The Goofers
David Frost
Shields & Yarnell
Tony Curtis
Carroll O'Connor
Murillo & Ulysses
Jeff Foxworthy
Lance Burton
Gus & His Friends
Jeff Dunham
Fred Travelina
Melinda
Blue Man Group

TRAVELING NATIONAL BROADWAY SHOWS

Sweet Charity
Fiddler on the Roof
Hello Dolly
Anything Goes
Once upon a Mattress
Flower Drum Song
Mama Mia
Oklahoma!
Guys & Dolls
Damn Yankees
The Jersey Boys

My Fair Lady
Phantom of the
Opera
Rock of Ages
Starlight Express
Mame
Cirque du Soleil
Annie

**MUSICIANS
AS A
FEATURED ACT**

Henry Mancini
Burt Bacharach
Doc Severinsen
Louie Bellson
Al Hirt
Louis Armstrong
Ted Lewis
Mickey Finn Show
Dick Contino
Roger Williams
Jack Sheldon
Maynard Ferguson
Lionel Hampton
Eddy Peabody & His
Banjo
Myron Floren
Vido Musso
Henry Levine
Charlie Teagarden
Red Norvo

Buddy Rich
Si Zentner
Bobby Sherwood
Ishkabibble (Mervin
Brogue)
Lynrd Skynrd
Carlos Santana
Los Lobos
Herbie Hancock
Johnny Dankworth
Yo Yo Ma
B.B. King
Pete Fountain

**NATIONALLY
KNOWN
ORCHESTRAS
APPEARING
OVER THE YEARS**

Woody Herman
Stan Kenton
Harry James
Maynard Ferguson
Count Basie
Duke Ellington
Tommy Dorsey
Charlie Barnet
Si Zentner
Dick Stabile
Ray Anthony
Guy Lombardo
Horace Heidt
Big Tiny Little

Tex Beneke
Glenn Miller
Les Brown
Jimmy Dorsey
Xavier Cugat
Les & Larry Elgart
Benny Goodman
Russ Morgan
Ted Weems
Buddy Rich
Jerry Gray
Ralph Marterie
Freddy Martin
Blue Barron
Jan Garber
Chuck Cabot
Don Ellis
Billy May
Ted FioRito
Mariachi Kings of
Mexico
Mongo Santamaria
Garwood Van
Dukes of Dixieland
Los Blues
Turk Murphy
Sam Donahue
Louis Jordan

MY THANKS

A HUGE DEBT OF GRATITUDE is owed to the many unnamed musicians who, along with myself, want to share and preserve some of the funny events and stories in musicians' lives.

A big vote of thanks also, is due my mentor, Thom Pastor, a fine musician and for many years the Secretary-Treasurer of Musicians Union, Local #369 in Las Vegas. Thom's thoughtful guidance and encouragement made it possible for many of these stories to be aired for the first time in the union's official paper, "The Desert Aria."

I owe a large amount of credit to my daughter, Lisa, whose insight made my efforts with this book much easier. Her knowledge of correct punctuation helped immensely.

Lastly, but certainly not least, to my soulmate wife, Kathleen, who, in her enormous role as editor-in-chief/ number one proof reader/ main copy reader and advisor, has valiantly suffered through countless retellings of these stories, I offer an enormous amount of thanks.

ABOUT THE AUTHOR

AFTER GRADUATING from Arizona State University with a degree in music education, John immediately began his 60-year career of playing professionally by going on the road with the internationally known bands of Woody Herman, Tommy Dorsey, and Buddy Morrow.

Over thirty-three of these years were spent in the showbands of Las Vegas performing more than 20,000 shows with major stars of the entertainment world.

In his many appearances as guest speaker for civic groups, music associations, and club meetings he relates interesting facts and experiences in professional music.

With his wife, Kathleen, John now lives in northern Colorado where he continues to actively play in several musical groups.

Made in the USA
Middletown, DE
01 May 2024

53699744R00099